KARL KERÉNYI

ATHENE: VIRGIN AND MOTHER

A Study of Pallas Athene

Translated from German by Murray Stein

1978

Spring Publications
Postfach
8024 Zürich
Switzerland

ACKNOWLEDGEMENTS

Acknowledgements for quotations from other authors have been made in the appropriate places in the text by the translator. The translation was made by Murray Stein from *Die Jungfrau und Mutter der Griechischen Religion: Eine Studie über Pallas Athene* by Karl Kerényi, Albae Vigiliae, N.F. Heft XII, Rhein Verlag, Zürich, 1952. The book was designed and composed by Susan Haule, helped by Caroline Weening, Robert Weening, John Haule, Chris Merritt, and the index by Lela Fischli. Mrs. Magda Kerényi gave generously of her time to help with many fine points.

The configuration of Athene, Erichthonios and Ge has been adapted from a detail of the Attic red figure cup by the Kodros painter, 430-420 B.C.; Berlin-Charlottenburg, F 2537, *CVA Berlin 3, plate 113,1, detail.* Cover design by Doris Oesch.

ISBN 0-88214-209-7

Composed, Photo-offset, and Manufactured in Switzerland by Buchdruckerei Schrumpf, 8123 Ebmatingen-Zürich, for Spring Publications, Postfach, 8024 Zürich.

All Spring Publications are also available in the United States from:
Spring, Box 1, Univ. of Dallas, Irving, Texas, 75061.

CONTENTS

Now would be the time for Gods to step forth
From inhabited things. . .
And embrace every wall
In my house. New page. Only the wind,
Flinging such a leaf into change,
Would suffice to blow up the air like soil:
A new breathing-field. Oh, Gods! Gods!
You often-come, sleepers in things,
Who resurrect gaily, who at the well
Which we imagine bathe throat and face,
And who easily add their restedness
To that which seems full, our full lives.
Once more let it be your morning, Gods.
We repeat. You alone are primal source.
With you the world arises, and a fresh start gleams
On all the fragments of our failures. . .

. . . I grasp nothing in the life of the Gods (which in the spirit most probably ever renews itself and runs its course and has its truth) so much as the moment in which they withdraw themselves: what would be a God without the cloud which preserves him? what would be a worn-out God?

Rainer Maria Rilke: *Sämtliche Werke, Vol. II,* p. 185;
and his letter to the Fürstin Marie von Thurn und Taxis,
23.9.1911 (Murray Stein translations).

ATHENE: VIRGIN AND MOTHER

The historical life of the Gods is played out between two poles, which are described in the foregoing quotation by someone who has not only reflected on them but has experienced them. Whoever has thought about this seriously can do nothing but refer to the poet who has, at the very least, gone through the threshold of the experience of the Gods. Both poles are boundary markers, which historical research comes up against at the beginning and end of its potentiality and validity.

The initial pole is where the Gods "step forth/ From inhabited things" – or from uninhabited things as well, if indeed there are such in a world that is of human beings. The final pole is where "they withdraw themselves." "The life of the Gods" between these two poles is that which "in the spirit ever renews itself and runs its course and has its truth." This life does not signify the completion, or even the repeated completion, of a biography, but rather an efficacious "now" that plays its variations in imagistic happenings. The richly varied play within the spirit is called mythology. The theater of mythology – the stage, the players, and the audience – is the human being. As with fabric, the Gods clothe themselves with him. From the historical perspective, they exist only in the material which has been woven from human beings themselves and from their surrounding world. Once they have stepped into this material – "material" understood as "clothing" – their *history* begins.

For this reason, the stories of the Gods have so much to do with *human* history. While the divinity of the Gods cannot be further penetrated, the human fabric is more analyzable. But we are after all concerned with the heroes of that history, with the Gods. They form the presupposition of mythology as they do of every historical study of them, of every "history of the Gods," and in all such cases it is never certain at the outset whether it is not more the history of attrition then the history of development, in the sense of a "spiritualization," or a combination of both. A Greek God comes to us in such manifold forms, from so many places, out of so many levels of past human life, that we must first of all assemble him as we would a heap of collected bones – which is itself a mythological act. But this is a difficult scientific procedure, not less so than that of archeologists, and it has similar prerequisites: a feeling for style, a feeling for structure and for the unique and special – for archeology the unique and special elements of works of art and artifacts, for us the unique and special elements of the Gods and the Divine. Particularity is just as timeless as structure. Stylistic differences are here also imagistic differences which characterize different archeological and human levels: the dimension of history is announced in these – and rendering insufficient the structure as a mere skeletal structure – a dimension which always leads back to the "hero" or "heroine" of the story who are not themselves merely structures. They are something more on the order of "forms of being" as Walter F. Otto conceives them, yet such as "bathe throat and face" – if not at our visible cisterns – and clothe themselves in human material. I have yet to mention the sensitivity for this material, for the concretely human; this could just as well be primary.

The reader is going to have to traverse a path of research which is not easy or familiar, not even for experts in the field. No thesis, no dogma of any kind of religion or philosophy – which would state how a God should be or not be, what he should be, or to what he should be reduced – not even the dogma of many scholars of religion who hold a preconceived notion that a God should evolve out of something and how he should develop, forms the basic plan of this path. Only the readiness to pay attention to how the pieces fit together is assumed. This was my method also in earlier mythological studies, even in my *The Gods of the Greeks*. It is a methodology which I was unable to discuss with critics who believed, at least before the appearance of that work, that this method was fundamentally determined by psychology. In this they proved their inexperience with this unique material which makes its own laws. It will be a pathway through undergrowth and piles of stones, through literary traditions and ruins – certainly through the ruins of the Acropolis of Athens. It will not be a simple pleasure, like reading the recounted tales of mythology which are told for their own sake.

One may read the mythology of Pallas Athene in my book *The Gods of the Greeks* in connection with this study. The "assembling" of the Goddess Athene must take place also on the basis of her *cultic* monuments: mythology and cult yield the *religion* of Pallas Athene. Cult – namely, as it is artfully worked out and built up through *rites* – is considered from the viewpoint of mythology: it is the exteriorization of the inner theater into a world theater, with the limitation placed on it that it can include only those aspects of inner experience which can be expressed in acts, yet including the supra-human which is "inhabited" by the human. Through such, man attains his just claim and his profit. For this reason psychologists have acknowledged the significance of cult for human beings far more than have the authors of materially more important works in the science of religion and ethnology, who are trapped in childish-magical power conceptions.

"If only we still had ceremonies, this treasure, which the most primitive aboriginals still have!" These are the words which one who is experienced in the creativeness of the soul, Max Kommerell, allows a modern psychologist to speak in his whimsically titled but historically and intellectually significant novel, *Der Lampenschirm aus drei Taschentüchern* (Berlin, 1940)

> Everything unadmitted thirsts for them. Perhaps there is a secret passion between daughter and father... I once saw two noble souls pale and shrink with fear and shame, instead of allowing the soothing divine hand of the father to establish the ceremonies which moderate wish-fulfillment into ritual celebration... That which exists, but does not actually happen, would have been stilled into a kiss, the touch of lip and forehead. This would have allowed great things to pass between them, and they would have enjoyed themselves innocently in the enthusiasm for conversation and song. Instead of feeling fear about approaching one another, they would have not begrudged their passion a series of festivals which end in memory.

No festival or cult – that is, no festival or cult in the real sense – was ever founded for the relationship of persons to persons without the Divine, which is the presupposition of the religious phenomena of "festival" and "cult," being experienced in it. There have been and are ceremonies of love and friendship. The same is true of love poems and poems of friendship, but they are truly poems only as they become elevated into the realm of art. Similarly there are festivals of love and friendship, but they are *proper festivals* and *proper cults* only when they have been elevated to the sphere of the Gods. This is the form in which the history of religions finds them. That they were initially elevated to this level without being initially directed at any God or at anything divine is neither demonstrable nor probable. The therapeutic meaning of cult, its healing and wholeness-creating power, is undeniable. We must procede from the fact that the cult is in history above all a *cultus deorum*, a cult of the Gods, with the emphasis not falling on the element of plurality.

I am presenting here, then, with grateful acknowledgment to everything I have learned from psychology (to learn, I believe, is less shameful than to exclude oneself from learning), a study in the history of religions. I would rather call it a study in "the history of the Gods" – the science of religion knows, after all, "studies in the history of ideas" – because it concerns the object of the cult and not the behavior expressed within the cult. Should virginal natures find self-recognition in it, this small book is dedicated also to them. What counts, above all, is the Goddess herself, who represents a still far-from-exhausted theme in the study of religion and antiquity, and whose presentation here is meant to be followed later by a larger set of associations into which it will fall. What was already completed before the appearance of *The Gods of the Greeks* is here made public; it is as much a preliminary study for that work as an aid for its understanding. *Albae Vigiliae* was founded for such preliminary studies. The reader should not feel disappointed if he finds himself being guided through the erected skeleton of a future construction.

Ponte Brolla, Switzerland, 27 May 1952

1

Probably the most human systematization of a mythology is that which came about through the constitution of the Olympian family of Gods. This happened through an historical process whose presupposition was that the more patriarchal Zeus religion and the more matriarchal Hera religion would encounter one another in the context of this family.[1] Within the sovereign dominion of the Mistress of the Heraion in Argos and of the kings of Mycenae, Greek *mythology* receives its ordering principle, through the association into which *Hera* entered with Zeus. Greek *religion*, however, is characterized much more through the high rank and position of another Great Goddess, Pallas Athene.

This does not mute the dominant patriarchal disposition of the Divine Family, so well-known from Homer. An earthly family, too, in which a daughter of the father – of the father only and not also of his wife –

played the leading role after the father and beside his wife, would nonetheless count as a patriarchal family. Granted, this would not be an ideal family of father-right, wherein the third place (after the spouse-and-queen) and in some cases even the second place (ahead of the first spouse) would be occupied by the son and heir to the throne. In Homer this second position is given to Pallas Athene. In a strict religious formula, which is a frequently recurring prayerful invocation of the three major Deities of the Greeks, Athene is named after Zeus, and Apollo is named third:[2]

> *Ai gar Zeu te pater kai Athēnaiē kai Apollon*
> When then, Oh father Zeus and Athene and Apollo...

This trinity of father-daughter-son would exist even without Hera. The Divine Patriarchy, which is an historical fact of Greek religion, is corrected from the viewpoint of a human ideal when Hector adds the missing spouse. He wishes the Divine Couple were his parents and his own rank that of those two which the previous prayer named: [3]

> If I could only be called son of Zeus of the aegis
> all the days of my life, and the lady Hera my mother,
> and I be honoured, as Apollo and Athene are honoured...

The cult of Hera remained locally characterized[4] on the one hand; on the other, it was tied to specific times of human life: to the time of wedding, to the times in the feminine life-cycle generally which made possible or impossible the encounter between wife and husband.[5] In contrast, a survey of the major locations of the Athene cult gives the impression that this Goddess belonged to the common property of the Greek race altogether differently than did Hera. Athene seems to be equally primary, if not equally prominent, everywhere.[6] So self-evident to all Greeks was her high rank that it did not have to be emphasized at every opportunity. The cult of Hera is more precisely fixed geographically, much more tied to particular shrines. Moreover, these shrines are dedicated exclusively to the Goddess as Protectress of a specific, feminine area of life, even though whole cities and islands, including both women and men, and these latter not only for their roles as husbands, submit themselves to her. This is a venerable heritage from pre-Greek, probably from neolithic, times.[7] The cultic places of Athene belong to the peaks of a wider realm, not only feminine and not only inclusive of married life. They exist mostly as shrines of a fortress and city Goddess. This too is a heritage from pre-Greek times. The early history of Athene has been traced back as far as the armed Protectress of the lords of Mycenean times and beyond that, though somewhat summarily, to the serpent-holding Protectress of the Minoan palaces on Crete.[8] The arms of shield and lance, the worship in more or less lofty and heavily fortified strongholds, the connections with bronze-casting and highly developed metallurgy, with the working of wool and with the harnessing of horses, are stylistic elements which characterize the Greek, and especially the Athenian, cult of Pallas Athene. And they appear as early as Mycenean culture. The serpent and steer, with which Athene was likewise connected,[9] belong to still more ancient times (this is mentioned here merely in an introductory fashion and will be expanded later).

Pallas Athene is a much richer, more complex and enigmatic divine figure than is Hera, the "Divine Wife." Were the puzzle once solved, along with the stories surrounding it, its mystery would still not disappear. Perhaps it is the mystery of Greek antiquity itself, whose historical development advanced, as it seems, under the sign and under the, let us say, protection of this Goddess. In contrast to the natural periodicity of Hera, the image of Athene contains a polarity and an inner tension which one cannot assert *a priori* was an accidental product of history. A friend of Goethe's, with whose thought and formulations he had much in common during his Roman period, Karl Philipp Moritz, first described and called attention to that tension and polarity. Pallas was for him "the wounder and healer, the destroyer and creator; the Goddess who delights in the turmoil of arms and in stormy, pitched battle, yet instructs man in the arts of weaving and of pressing oil from the olive."[10] Another observer of Pallas in Goethe's time also saw the inner antitheses, and in these he saw a problem that needed to be resolved: "It was and still is very common to consider Athene the Goddess of Wisdom, even though it is not easy to understand how as such she could have become associated with the deeds of a war Goddess. But if one looks upon her as a war Goddess, as a symbol of martial bravery combined with sagacity and cunning, one cannot easily understand why such a divinity was not conceived of in a masculine form, nor what she would have had in common with the arts of peace."[11]

The solution recommended by this old monograph on Athene should be at least summarily cited here, since it sketches a unified image which one will perhaps gladly look back to during the following reconstructive study. Whoever surveys the multifaceted forms of the Goddess's cult, it claims, will be led to the conviction that it was all-mighty divine Power, Wisdom, and Goodness, in short Divine Providence, which the Greeks worshipped as the mighty, high-minded, gracious daughter of the Lord of Heaven, as Pallas Athene. From this center radiated the whole variety of the Goddess's traits and achievements; toward this center are directed all of her epithets, symbols, customs, and cultic celebrations, all of her associations and relations to other Gods, all of her mythical deeds. The Heavenly Power above all else had to appear as a Protectress into whose care one could commend oneself with pious trust in those peaceless, war-filled times when the only rule that held was "might makes right." The Strong, the Valiant, the Defender, she protects cities and fortresses from hostile invasions and harbors from hostile landings. She holds her hand outstretched over cities and covers them with her golden shield; she watches over them with a reconnoitering, spirited, menacing gaze. Amidst the inspiring noise of trumpets and flutes she leads the army to victory, glory, and booty. Militant warriors favor her above all the Gods. She is the strong, unvanquished, virginal Goddess, and her image, the Palladium, guarantees security for the city and for the besieged a sacred place of refuge whose desecration by force is fiercely punished by her fierce anger.

She is the rescuer from every danger and peril, the advisor for every tight spot, and the highest wisdom. The people's chiefs and leaders, as well as the whole people itself, are advised by her; she presides over all local, tribal, and national gatherings. She maintains life and health. She is the gracious, gentle nurse who takes the children of mankind to herself, who makes mothers fertile and children grow and develop, who increases the stock of the people through a strong younger generation. She preserves the divine order in nature, protects the seedlings and fruits from damage, sows and tends the noble and nourishing olive trees; she teaches men how to manufacture the plow, how to yoke oxen, and how to loosen up the hard ground with the rake. From her mankind receives the materials for all the arts that beautify life, and from her the metal workers and the arms-smiths, the housewives and weavers, receive their skillfulness. She gave mankind the bridle so that he could master the horse for his own use. Shipbuilders work under her inspiration. She is enthroned protectively on the headlands, stirring up and stilling the storms. To her the sailor offers thanks as he happily steps to land at his desired goal. She guides the wanderer and the stranger safely over sea and land, and she accompanies the heroes on their adventures, fills them with courage, and saves them from danger. But she is also righteous, strictly recompensing Providence: seated beside Zeus, she is the only one who knows where the lightning bolts lie hidden, has the full right and power to use them, and also employs the aegis, the terrible shield of her father Zeus. With him she has many traits and epithets in common, and she is frequently worshipped jointly with him, especially in the most ancient sites of her cult.

From the viewpoint of the history of religions, it is necessary to strip away the Christian coloration of this presentation and especially to disregard the reference to Providence, a concept that was connected with the Goddess only very late. Yet, even so, the agreement between a purely spiritual conception of Pallas Athene and our oldest sources remains remarkable. Hesiod places the Goddess on an equal footing with Zeus insofar as courage and wise counsel are concerned.[12] In this respect he does not contradict Homer, who places Athene second in the significant trinity of Zeus-Athene-Apollo. The testimony of Hesiod's *Theogony* states with even more historical clarity than do the Homeric passages that in Greece the religion of Athene, next to that of the Zeus religion and above that of the Apollo religion, had the most provisions for existing as a spiritual religion which penetrated into every aspect of life. Although it was the religion of a Goddess, it actually existed side by side with the victorious father religion, in no respect subordinated to it as was the naturalistic Hera religion, but in all practical respects equal to it, yet without overthrowing the general patriarchal order. Is this not really an accidental product of history? But then one must also ask whether history could have produced such a thing without there being some foundation for it in the structure of human beings. If merely the result of historical accident, would this position of the Goddess have been acceptable, and would her image itself, with its internal tension and antitheses, which soon will appear to us to be even stronger, have been tolerable?

2

From the very first the mythology of Athene seems to contradict every human analogy. In what sort of family is it conceivable that a daughter be born without a mother? That she sprang forth from the head of her father? Such a miraculous birth is presented already by Homer and told by Hesiod, and from a purely theoretical standpoint it suits an absolutely patriarchal order better than would a natural birth. But only theoretically, since the mythologem assumes no human proportionality whatsoever.

Considered from the viewpoint of that beautiful anthropomorphism, the epiphany in human form, which the Greeks preferred in every other appearance of the Divine, this one contains such a grotesque conception that one must wonder how it could have held its ground despite the prevailing views of Homer and of those after him. [13] The closest analogy to this conception stems from the archaic mythology of the Polynesians. [14] There a similar story is told, not about a God but about a primal Goddess. The Earth Mother, having been impregnated by the Sky Father, gave birth to the God of fishes and reptiles through her arm, or "directly through the head." Archaic mythologies do also show, then, a kind of anthropomorphism in which prior events that are not thought of in anthropomorphic terms, such as here the origin of fishes and reptiles, are presented in the form of human, though not humanly normal, events.

The mother is not completely missing from the mythologem of the miraculous birth of Pallas Athene. According to Hesiod's account of the weddings of Zeus, whose sequential ordering is most likely the invention of the poet of the *Theogony*, [15] the King of the Gods chose Metis as his first wife. She was of all beings "the most knowing" [16] (as the word *mētis* is interpreted), or "of many counsels" as translated in the sense of the Homeric epithet *polymētis.* As she was about to give birth to the Goddess Athene, Zeus deceived his pregnant wife with cunning words and assimilated her into his own body. Mother Earth and Father Sky had advised him to do this so as to prevent any of his descendants from robbing him of his kingly rank. For it was destined that the most brilliant children were to be born to the Goddess Metis: first, the daughter Athene, and later a son, the future King of Gods and men. Hesiod, following the patriarchal line of thought, bases this inhuman, non-anthropomorphic deed of Zeus – swallowing his wife – upon the fear for the son, heir to the throne. Yet even here the viewpoint of mother-right retains some of its force. The feared heir to the throne is to be born from a particular mother. This motif, wherever it appears in mythology or heroic saga, betrays matriarchal thinking. Not even the extremely unfeminine father's daughter, Pallas Athene, is born to the father alone. Even she has a mother who carries her to term within the body of Zeus and enables and forces the devouring husband to deliver the child.

It is unlikely that this mythologem was invented by Hesiod; even less can it be considered a later addition to the *Theogony*.[17] It is archaic in every detail. A Hittite text may be cited as an archaic analogy to the devouring of Metis.[18] What happened between the Gods Anu and Kumarbi in a purely masculine line bespeaking an absolutely patriarchal mode of thought is the same as took place here between Metis and Zeus where the maternal source within the patriarchal order is recognized: as the pregnant mother is devoured here, there the semen-bearing member of the father was devoured so that the devouring son would be fertile. The close kinship, perhaps even the common origin of these two mythologems explains how Metis in the texts of the Orphics, which retained the archaic elements as much as possible,[19] can also be masculine and – as is stated literally[20] – "bear the famous seed of the Gods."

Hesiod lists the Goddess Metis among the daughters of Okeanos and Tethys,[21] as he did also others among the Great Goddesses of ancient times. Also speaking against the view that Metis and her mythologem are to be seen as relatively late products, is the Attic tale which knows of a royal line of Metionidai. The name of the ancestral progenitor, Metion, assumes descent from Metis as the originator of the line, and with this assumes also a matriarchal mode of thought. The mythological existence of Metis is proven here independently of Hesiod through the fact that she was given another mother, not Tethys but Daidale, who through this non-Hesiodian geneology became the grandmother of Athene.[22] The connection between Metis and Pallas Athene, however, certainly existed already by the time Daidale was introduced into the geneology. The craftsmen who were represented by Daidalos, to whose art the name Daidale points, stood under the protection of the daughter of Zeus, and this is how Daidale entered the geneology. Metis, the Goddess of "wise counsel," bears an abstract name which may be as pre-Hesiodian as the name Eros, "the love claim."[23] Pallas Athene cannot be reduced to the concept "wise counsel," although one of her aspects is expressed through this attribute, i.e., her *spiritual* aspect, which in the form of Metis shows itself to be more *maternal* than virginal.

3

It is a characteristic feature of Greek religion that the Goddesses, who make up a significant number of venerable maternal and virginal forms, maintain an equal balance with the masculine supremacy among the Gods. Preeminently this is done by Pallas Athene: as no other, she is the daughter of her father, the Highest God, and unites virgin and mother in one and the same divine Person. In the cult of Hera, who again and again becomes virginal in order to offer her virginity to her divine Husband, and who bears children, children without a father, one awaits in vain the epithet "mother." This cultic epithet is also absent from Artemis, even though in Asia Minor she was identical to the Great Mother. In Greece she never signified "mother."[24] Precisely this contrast with Artemis, whose cults were sometimes most unchaste,[25] demonstrates how significant it is that Pallas Athene was worshipped in both aspects: as Parthenos, in the sense of a chaste, almost masculine maiden, and as mother. In Greece the relation to sex is not exhausted by the alternatives of chastity and unchastity. There are many combinations and mixtures: "chaste" is not always identical with "virginal," nor even with "temperate." The study of religion must go beyond the general concept of "cultic chastity," as also beyond the abstract concept of "fertility," if it is to avoid gross simplification. The question always arises as to what is supposed to be understood concretely by these concepts. In the case of Athene one has the opportunity, first of all, to speak more concretely about the phenomenon of fertility.

If the chorus of old Athenian men[26] addresses the Goddess as "Mother, Mistress, and Protectress," one might suppose that she were named "Mother" in an unusual, or perhaps a merely poetical, sense. The Athene Meter of the Elis cult, however, bore this epithet as Goddess of motherhood in the truest sense. She brought about conception, which was not simply the self-evident and inevitable result of men uniting with women; and she entered this realm, which from the viewpoint of Hera must be looked at in a completely different light,[27] not only for the sake of fertility. According to cultic legend,[28] the women of Elis once prayed to the Goddess, when all the men of suitable age had left the country, that they might conceive immediately upon being reunited with their men. Because this prayer was granted, they founded the temple to "Mother Athene"; and because the men and women had particularly enjoyed their reunion, they named the place where it happened and the stream that ran in front of the place Bady, which means "sweet." The action of Athene is given here a different *telos*, a different meaning for the love union than this union receives in Hera's sphere of action. Here *conception* belongs to fulfillment; in the ideational world of mother-right, on the other hand, which was attached to the wife of Zeus, not obvious motherhood but the woman's *completion* through the man is sought for and found – this is a viewpoint that may be called matriarchal. The fulfillment that may be attained only in being *impregnated* by the man signifies the subordination of the woman to a higher goal, namely, the securing of offspring, and for this reason it conceals within itself a typical *patriarchal* standpoint.

As it appears in connection with Athene, motherhood must be understood in terms of father-right. For this there is a late but nonetheless valuable testimony in the privileged city of the Goddess.[29] In Athens the priestess of Athene visited the newly married women wearing the aegis, the sacred goatskin, which had been removed from the cultic statue. As such she appeared as the representative of the Goddess,[30] and because – not being a virgin herself but a married woman[31] – she mediated a sort of epiphany of Athene and placed the new marriage under the protection of the existing patriarchal order. This order above all else required descendants. The occasion for this ceremony[32] was the common wedding celebration for all the couples who had married during the year. It was probably no different in Elis. The meeting of all women and men at a stream – the stream- or river-God played a role precisely in wedding rites in Greece[33] – probably takes the place of the annual communal wedding festival.

In her character as "Mother," Athene was above all a wedding Goddess, though not in the same sense as Hera. The evidence suggests a middle stage between the order of mother-right, as this is reflected in the cult and mythology of Hera, and the patriarchal world in Greece. Three stages of Greek cultural and religious history are evident. This conclusion is reached independently of Bachofen's schema[34] and without reliance on broad generalizations. One can find analogies in other places, but the Greek conditions, insofar as they allow for reconstruction from the concrete Greek materials, are at least equally instructive from the general human point of view. The transitional stage between the orders of mother-right and father-right was characterized in Greece by male societies, which in the course of history more and more lost their character (well-known in ethnology) as secret societies. What remained in the end were classifications of men into "brotherhoods," the phratries. In this final, purely formal condition, the phratriai of Athens had practically no other task than assuming responsibility for the early maturational ceremonies, by now very faded in form, for young boys at the feast called Apaturia, and then for leading them step by step toward the stage of marriage.[35] They also registered the marriageable maidens and accepted them into the phratrie as wives.[36] As Phratria and Apaturia, Athene is the Goddess of these ancient male societies. Among the male Deities, Zeus Phratrios stands in the first position beside her.[37] Hephaistos was especially revered among them,[38] being also a "marriage candidate" for Pallas Athene. We will often meet representatives of the male sex in the realm of this virginal, and in a special way also maternal, Goddess. For now, just one particularly instructive example has been selected.

There is the cultic legend from a small island not far from Athens, across from Troezen.[39] Appearing as an apparition, Athene sent the maiden Aithra there, where she could be taken by Poseidon, or in another tradition by Aigeus. Having celebrated her involuntary wedding, which had been desired by the Goddess, she founded a temple there to Athene Apaturia and gave the island a new name. Earlier the island had been called Sphairia, "the round," but since that event it was called Hiera, "the holy." This legend explains the custom of the Troezen maidens offering their girdles to Athene Apaturia before their weddings. For this purpose they went to the holy island. The Athenian maidens, too, were led by their parents to the Acropolis on the day before their weddings in order to make an offering to Athene.[40] Athene protectively surrounds the wedding event with her presence and secures the conception of a child. In the heroic legend this had to do with an heroic child: Aithra became the mother of Theseus. What is striking in this is the importance attached to conception, which highlights the patriarchal viewpoint within the Athene-inspired union.

In the antique tradition there are explicit testimonies of a certain amount of consciousness about the transition which took place under the protection of Athene. The transition from the matriarchal mode of thought (that left fatherhood to incalculable powers) to the patriarchal order, which consecrated specific institutions to conception and thereby concretized fatherhood, was expressed in the language of the saga, that primal mythological history of Athens. During the period when the Goddess seized possession of her property on Attic soil, when she struggled for it against Poseidon and single-handedly fortified the Acropolis,[41] there reigned there the earth-born, half-serpent primal man Kekrops, the first king of Athens: this is the one "of whom it may be said that he first revealed the two elements of origination, the father and mother."[42] This remarkable assertion was supposed to explain the epithet for Kekrops, *diphuēs,* with a different strand of the saga than the fantastic one that he had a two-fold form, which is what the word actually means. This less fantastic, but by no means obvious, explanation was further substantiated by the assumption of general promiscuity in primal times, in which the father had to remain anonymous; to counter this Kekrops would have introduced monogamy. In this pseudo-historical construction of a rationalistic era – it originates with the historian Klearch[43] – there thus appears, as an element of the explanation, a tradition of the introduction of the patriarchal order. In agreement is another tradition contained in the form of a saga, according to which women, under the reign of Kekrops, lost the right to name children after their mothers, i.e., metronymically and not patronymically.[44]

Kekrops belongs to Pallas Athene not only in saga; he is also bound to her in cult. His tomb is alleged to have been located in the sanctuary of the Goddess on the Acropolis, which was named the Erechtheion after Erechtheus, another kingly worshipper of Athene who was born from the earth and later transformed into a serpent. Both of these kings who were connected with Athene have archaic outward forms, which in the same temple were objects of religious veneration,[45] concretely as animals – i.e., as the "home-protecting serpent" (*oikouros ophis*). In Attica, however, Zeus too bore the form of serpent as Meilichios[46] – an epithet of the paternal God of the underworld, as well as of Dionysos in this aspect – and as Ktesios, who is mentioned with Athene Ktesia in one and the same prayer formula.[47] In the rich theriomorphism of the mythology of Pallas Athene, the association of the Goddess with the form of the serpent certainly belongs to the most ancient stratum. The assertion is even put forward that the serpent – at once "palace snake" and "Palace Goddess" – was the prehistoric predecessor of the Goddess herself.[48] On the Acropolis of Athens it appears as the masculine complement to the Fortress Goddess, as the most archaic in the line of masculine beings whose most ancient representatives had the form of serpent, or took on the serpent form, or like Zeus removed it by degrees: the primal kings Kekrops and Erechtheus and the divine child Erichthonios As the closest analogue one thinks of a similar role for the serpent in the case of the Minoan "Palace Goddess," particularly if one avoids its relation to the sphere of fertilization. The possibility of a mythical wedding of serpents, in which the bride would also take the form of serpent, must naturally be considered in this connection. As one can infer from the Orphic tradition, such a mythologem exists in connection with Rhea and Zeus, mother and son, as a prelude to a second serpent wedding between Zeus and Persephone, father and daughter, wherein only the masculine portion of the incest – and therefore very archaical – pair appeared in animal form.[49] A prehistoric serpent cult and serpent mythology, which most likely had their early forms in Crete and their analogies in Egypt and in still more southern, snake-infested lands, project themselves into the Attic cult of Athene, not amorphously however, but in the form of archaic mythologems. Over against the mother-son mythologem, which is connected to Crete through the image of Rhea, the patriarchal tone of the Athene religion creates something definitely new; it creates nothing new, however, in relation to the father-daughter mythologem. Despite this, however, a graduated transition does become evident.

Within the cultic domain of Athene, the serpent is the complement of the maternal aspect of the Goddess and simply refers to the fertilizing masculine sphere, to the father and to his continuation, the son. Another tradition points in the same direction. The same Kekrops, whose respect-commanding authority as arbiter in the dispute between Athene and Poseidon provides evidence that he belongs to a more ancient stratum of religion and culture in Attica than the disputing Deities themselves; this serpentine partner of the Goddess, who in the realm of the Athene religion also plays the role of husband and father, was also according to Athenian tradition supposed to have introduced the patriarchal Zeus- and Athene-cult. He is supposed to have first given a name to Zeus and to have first erected a statue to Athene;[50] perhaps more precisely he was the first to name Zeus "Hypatos" ("the highest").[51] This epithet is the first to allow the patriarchal Sky God in Zeus to step forward fully. In nearby Marathon it was precisely in the marriage month of Gamelion that sacrifice was made to Hypatos.[52]

4

We devoted the foregoing reflections to the *maternal* side of Pallas Athene, also to the strong *patriarchal emphasis* in her image. The first act of the Hesiodian birth narrative, the marriage and pregnancy of Metis (Goddess of wise counsel), receives what must now be considered unquestionable corroboration through the facts of the cult of Athene Meter and through stories such as the marriage and pregnancy of the Athene priestess Aithra: the terms "Metis" and "Mother" describe an aspect of Pallas Athene herself. How does this relate to the patriarchal, maidenly aspect of the Goddess, to the classical image of the *virginal* Athene?

It has been maintained that this is the result of a relatively late development, with the "Parthenos" seen as entering the picture as the Greeks moved through a refinement of taste toward classicism: "Parthenos" replaced "Meter" without being able wholly to suppress it.[53] Such a development presupposes that virginity would have enjoyed greater respect than motherhood in the high period of Greek history, particularly in Athens. But this is by no means the case. According to our sources, Athene is first addressed as "Mother" by Euripides, but this should not lead us to the false conclusion that she was not worshipped in this aspect earlier. The signs of the worship of the Mistress of the Acropolis in Athens as a maternal Goddess who was closer to women appear in her unarmed representations, above all in the work of Endoios – granting that the identification of the seated statue in the Acropolis Museum is correct. His statue creates a matronly effect, even though her bosom is bedecked with the aegis and the Gorgoneion – the frightening goatskin and the grotesque face.[54] The image of the armed, masculine-minded maiden is, however, also old, older than Homer for whom it is a given premise. The *arms*, the *virginity*, and the *masculine character* are expressed mythologically as direct descent from the father – these three elements together present a unified, unmistakeable, distinct totality.

The worship of a divine Virgin does not suggest a later style on Greek soil than worship of a divine Mother. To the enduring residue of ancient Cretan mythology belongs the image of the "sweet virgin" Britomartis, called by this name in the pre-Greek language of the great island.[55] On the northern periphery of the Greek world, on the Black Sea and in Thrace, there is evidence for the cult of a Goddess no more specifically named than "Parthenos," who was comparable to the warlike maiden Athene.[56] This Goddess, who judging from the style of her cult was "barbaric" (i.e., remained archaic), was equated with Artemis, and with Athene on the island of Lemnos and on the Bosphorus, where she bore the name Chryse.[57] The virginity of a Goddess is therefore certainly not the product of a relatively late and exclusively Greek development. In the case of the Thracian-Pontic Parthenos, this feature is so strongly emphasized and placed in the foreground that a reason such as has been advanced to explain the virginity of the Greek Goddesses would hardly suffice. As this explanation has it, Goddesses who have their own well-defined meaning and function will not tolerate husbands beside them. They are much too independent to be subordinated to a man. This is meant to be valid not only for Athene, but for Demeter, Artemis, Hestia, and even Aphrodite as well. Either they remain virginal, or they casually bind themselves to a God or to a hero and bear him a child if such suits their nature.[58]

In agreement with this conception, which justly stresses the particular, unmistakeable nature of the individual Goddesses, stands a noteworthy psychological conception of virginity. As this conception is formulated, the woman who is psychologically virginal is *independent*. She is what she is, fully apart from whether she even belongs to a man or not.[59] In itself it would be possible that such virginity, which is a form of feminine existence that can represent a valid experience of the soul, would have appeared to the Greeks as the defining characteristic of a Goddess. Above all others Aphrodite would come under consideration here. She, however, was considered by the Greeks precisely not to be a virgin. Of three other Goddesses, on the contrary, it is explicitly maintained that they never had anything to do with love: Athene, Artemis, and Hestia.[60] Of these only Hestia does not relate to another God in such a way that virginity could be explained as independence more than as the opposite of independence. The virginity of Goddesses such as Artemis and Athene, who are more clearly defined images than is Hestia, differs according to the nature of these divine Virgins and contains much more that is positive than merely the negativity implied by independence itself. In the instance of Artemis, it conceals in itself the untameable wildness of a particular age of maidenhood[61] along with the closest relationship to the brother; in the case of Athene, it contains the unconquerable determination of the masculinely oriented battle Goddess along with the closest relationship to the father.

It is the image of the armed and terrifying maiden that gets associated with the birth from the head of Zeus. The *Iliad* alludes to this mythologem. Ares reproaches Zeus for giving birth to such a daughter and describes at the same time her terrifying force in battle.[62] In his rage he gives her the epithet *aphrōn* ("crazed," "frantic"), by which he calls into question any association she might have to prudence and wise counsel. This means, though, that Athene's close connection to Metis was very familiar to the poet and to his audience. It was precisely at her epiphany from the head of the father that her quality as a Goddess of war came to the fore, and this is equally true in all three classical passages which testify to this form of birth. Hesiod, who at the beginning of his list of Zeus's spouses told of the swallowing of Metis, describes the epiphany at the conclusion of the list:[63]

> Then from his head, by himself,
> he produced Athene of the grey eyes,
> great goddess, weariless,[64]
> waker of battle noise, leader of armies
> a goddess queen who delights in war cries,
> onslaughts and battles.

Pindar authenticates another very vivid but also very unclassical and rather archaic feature of the mythologem, i.e., Hephaistos' help at the birth, which he effected through a blow to the head of Zeus with his crescent-moon ax.[65] Whereupon, "Athene sprang from the skull of Zeus with an earth-shattering battle-cry,[66] so that the heavens shook and the mother earth." The poet of the 28th Homeric Hymn, using the same poetic style, seeks to give the complete account. Present in his description, too, are the epithets associated with Metis. In this epiphany, however, the other martial aspect of Athene comes more clearly to the fore: she is born from the sacred head, clad in armor of resplendent gold; all the Gods are awed by her appearance as she leaps before aegis-bearing Zeus from his immortal head, brandishing the sharp-pointed spear; great Olympus quakes under the force of the owl-eyed Goddess; the earth all about resounds deeply and the sea heaves in an uproar of dark-colored waves; the ocean's tides burst over the shores, and for a long while, until Pallas Athene finally removes the divine armor from her shoulders, Hyperion's heavenly son allows the sun's horses to stand still. In conclusion the poet of the Hymn once more alludes to the Metis aspect, when he adds: "And Zeus the God repleat with wise counsel, rejoiced."

Belonging also to the martial aspect of Athene is her association with the war God Ares, an association that cannot be simply judged as one of enmity.

They are bound to one another also through rivalry, and Ares betrays his jealousy when he reproves Zeus for giving birth to this "foolish, dangerous daughter." The superiority is of course Athene's: as the two of them confront each other on the battlefield, the Goddess strikes her opponent with a boulder.[67] These are examples of a negative association. On the shield of Achilles, however, it was shown how Ares and Athene, a similarly disposed and constituted pair, jointly led forth the departing warriors.[68] One may speak of an ambivalent relationship: for Homer the rivalry weighs heavier, while in the cult the positive association is highlighted much more. In Attica Ares was the beloved of a figure who stood in a particularly close association to Athene: Aglauros. We are not completely informed about the secret love affair,[69] but we do know of an exact parallel, the identical case with a somewhat altered name: Tritaia, a priestess of Athene like Aithra and according to her name clearly a representative of Tritogeneia herself, became the divine Ancestress of the Achaean town of the same name after she bore to the war God the founder of the city, Melanippos.[70] From the association of Ares with Aglauros a daughter was born who was the exact double of her mother, yet with a name much like that of Melanippos ("he with the black stallion," or "a black stallion") belongs to a level of Greek mythology in which the horse rules as the characteristic animal. The mother, Aglauros, was connected to the serpent; the daughter, Alkippe, was according to her name like a courageous mare.

We will return later to the chronological deductions which follow from the fact that the association between Ares and Athene does not yet manifest in the symbol of the horse, at least not in Athens. The facts of the cult which remain still to be mentioned here indicate the association of the Goddess with Ares and with militant youth: the oath of arms of the Athenian Epheboi was sworn in the sanctuary of Aglauros, and during this ceremony the God of war was addressed by two names.[71] On the Areopagos, the hill across from the Acropolis, an altar was dedicated to Athene Areia –

the "Athene of Ares"[72] – and in the temple of Ares stood a statue of Athene and one of the battle Goddess Enyo, two related images. Through the first part of her name (derived from *alke*, "defensive power and courage," and from *alalkein*, "to defend"), Alkippe, who besides being the daughter of Aglauros was also the wife of Metion, the ancestor of the Metionidai,[73] was associated with a series of epithets for Athene which point to the north, in the direction of the Thracian-Pontic Parthenos: Alalkomene and Alalkomneis were the names of the Goddess in her Boeotian town of Alalkomenai, named after her,[74] and in her Macedonian town of Pella she was Alkidemos.[75] The weapons of the Goddess – helmet, lance, shield – serve both the purposes of defense and of frightening away, as do also the aegis and the Gorgoneion. In this, her frightening-away defensive aspect is allied with her maternal, protective aspect.

The discovery of a painted limestone plate in Mycenae bearing the representation of a shield-bearing Goddess and two feminine devotees testifies to the great age of this image and to its validity for Mycenaean culture.[76] Perseus as well, the hero and protégé of Athene with a pre-Greek, mythological name, belongs to the territory of this same culture. Against the opinion that this Mycenaean representation was the oldest image of Athene the objection was raised[77] that the painted plate actually shows practically only the powerful figure-8-formed shield, behind which the Goddess is hidden. One shield alone discloses very little of what Pallas Athene meant to the Greeks and nothing at all of the essence which we confront in the mythology of the Goddess and in her cults behind a continuously recurring duality of aspects. "Only the 'bright-eyed intelligence' capable of discerning the decisive element at every juncture and of supplying the most effective instrumentality is an adequate characterization of her ideal" – this is how Otto sought to grasp the essence of the Goddess. "Consummation, the immediate present, action here and now – that is Athene." Or again: "she is the spirited immediacy, redeeming spiritual presence, swift action. She is the *ever-near*."[78] These insights represent an advance in the understanding of the Goddess, beyond the concept which identified the Goddess with divine "Providence," and beyond the concept of a Mycenaean palace Goddess as well, which, while being historically valid, left it without religious content.

Otto's formulations still do not, however, give sufficient definition to the essential core of the rich manifestation that was the historical Pallas Athene. Even in Mycenaean times this manifestation may have been more multifaceted than the painting of that time could indicate. The quality of being "one who is ever near" and the Goddess of wise counsel belongs to a particular aspect of Athene, one that is not identical with the martial and virginal qualities. Hers is the sagacity of a *mother* who is completely focused on the father and oriented to *father-right*, a motherly sagacity that does not give itself arbitrarily to everyone. From the outside, at least since Mycenaean times, Athene was a fear-inspiring battle Goddess, but she had her favorite heroes, her favorite warriors, and her favorite towns, all of whom she guided with maternal care. The maternal associations are hidden behind the image of *martial maiden*, but they do not contradict it. The inner contradiction of the figure is nonetheless undeniable: it lies in the representation of a *virginal mother*.

5

As the theme of our further reflections we elect to pursue this established duality of aspects. Its appearance is not an accidental product of history. It is so characteristic of this Goddess that we could hardly even speak of Pallas Athene if only one or the other side stood before us without the tension and polarity of both. This is what differentiates a *Goddess*, who is able to exercise power over human beings, from a mere *personification*.

The duality finds expression in the name of Pallas Athene itself, and at least this much is certain: one of the two names portrays the martial and virginal aspect. The meaning of Pallas (*pallas*, of which the plural is *pallades*) is handed down to us, as is also its precise differentiation[79] from other words deriving from the same stem:[80] it was once the name for robust maidens and implied the meaning of the masculine word *pallas* (*pallantes* in the plural), "robust young man." A distinct masculinity seems to adhere to this word even in its feminine form. It is perhaps best repeated by the Latin *virago*. In Attica, saga told of a Pallas who was a "teacher of Giants," a hero after whom the land of Pallene was named and most likely himself a Giant.[81] The quality of the "gigantic," of fierce manliness, was distinctly evoked by the similar name of the Great Goddess of Attica and (especially) of Pallene. The derivative word Palladium refers to the statue of Athene as battle Goddess with lance poised and shield raised.[82] Athene is supposed to have created this statue by herself as a likeness of her companion Pallas, the daughter of her teacher Triton, whom she killed by mistake in a tournament[83] – a story which with others shows what a degree of independence one aspect of the Goddess could achieve.

Whether the feminine name "Pallas" especially accents the virginity of the divine Maiden cannot be stated with certainty. "Parthenos" and "Kore" also do not particularly stress this, but they certainly do refer to the *girlishness* of the Goddess concerned, whose characters are in turn indicated by particular mythologems – such as those of Hera Pais and Parthenos. In the case of the name Pallas, one has to associate with a *masculine* Pallas, with an extraction from androgynous unity; this would explain the androgeny of the Goddess. In fact, there are traces of an older mythologem, not contained in the classical mythology of the Greeks, which confirms the relationship of Pallas Athene to a masculine Pallas. The masculine partner of the Goddess usually bears this name and plays the role of father or teacher.[84] Classical mythology knows of several Pallantes, undisguised Giants, all of whom can probably be traced back to a single paternal image such as Atlas or the Sumerian Enlil, a gigantically powerful God who holds heaven and earth apart.

According to the Homeric Hymn to Hermes, Pallas, provided there with a father who is otherwise unknown,[85] was the father of the moon Goddess Selene. Hesiod's Pallas is a son of the Titan Krios, a brother of Astraios ("God of the stars"), and of the father of the moon Goddess Hecate, and himself the father of Zelos and Kratos, Bia and Nike.[86] This last Goddess is also known as Athene Nike, but the remaining siblings – "Zeal," "Strength," and "Might" – are also worthy of relationship to the indefatigable battle Goddess. An archaic winged God named Pallas – with wings attached to the ankles, or winged like the archaic winged Goddesses, among whom Athene herself may be numbered – was according to one tradition the father of Pallas Athene.[87] In the war against the Giants a certain Pallas confronted Athene and was killed by her; she even tore off his skin.[88] She did the same thing, however, to her father Pallas, who had lustfully seduced his own daughter.[89] The father-daughter mythologem is thus transmitted both through the masculine and feminine Pallas, not in the form of a serpent wedding but in that of a seduction scene between archaic Deities, probably two winged beings. The setting in the form of a war against the Giants is a dilution of this, suited to classical mythology. The saga of Pallas, son of Lykaon and founder of the Arcadian town Pallantion, represents a further dilution.[90] At this level Pallas is seen only as the teacher of Athene, yet still as father of Nike and Chryse, two manifestations of the Goddess herself.[91] At the same level of dilution the incest motif appears again, behind the lightly disguised name of the Goddess, but in the form of a consummated marriage between her and the "teacher." According to the Boeotian saga, from the realm of Athene Alalkomene or Alalkomeneis, the primal man Alalkomeneus reared Pallas Athene.[92] His wife is also mentioned: she was named Athenais.[93]

6

Can the name "Athene" or "Athenais, Athena" be referred to the motherly, "Metis" aspect of the Goddess as the name "Pallas" was to the father-bound, almost masculine, martial aspect? Of the two names, "Athene" (with its variations) is the more essential, the one which was established earlier as the exclusive proper name of the Goddess. Even Homer never says "Pallas" alone instead of "Pallas Athene" or "Pallas Athenaie," but he does use the second name without the first. A scrupulous sacred language expands the simple appellation of the Athenian city Goddess with a formula which leaves no room for doubt that this and no other "Athene" is intended: *Athēna ē Athēnōn medeousa*[94] (Athene, the Guardian of Athens). The old question, whether the town was named after "Athenai" after Athene, or vice versa, must be adjudicated in favor of the first alternative:[95] if "Athene" had originally signified merely the "Goddess of the town or fortress Athens," there would have been no need to refer to her as "Athene of Athens."

The Boeotian city of Alalkomenai was named after the martial aspect of the Goddess, after her epithet Alalkomene. Athenai, after the difficult-to-interpret name Athene, was the name not only of the city that was to achieve world-wide historical importance but also of an otherwise unknown place on the island of Euboia: Athenai Diades. The second name here stresses the relationship to Zeus, and in this may lie a distinction between the specific city Goddess who was the exclusive daughter of Zeus, and other city Goddesses of the same name who were bound as daughters (and not only as daughters) to a serpent God or to a winged God, before they too became daughters of Zeus. Just as it was possible for several "Pallades," "Parthenoi," "Korai" to be Goddesses, so it seems that several "Athenai," all of them city and fortress Goddesses, "Poliades," were worshipped before the great Daughter of Zeus came to be recognized as the only proper one.

An acceptable meaning for the word "Athene" is yielded only if one dares to reach for an old forgotten vocabulary, which in several instances has turned out to be the common property of the pre-Greek inhabitants of Greece and the Etruscans of Italy.[96] From the sacred language of the Etruscans have been preserved such words as *althanulus*, "holy vessel of the priest"; *atena*, "clay beaker for use in sacrifice";[97] *attana*, "pan."[98]

The signification of "a kind of vessel, a dish, beaker, or pan" will certainly appear at first glance to be less suited to a Goddess than the meaning of "Pallas." The reason that the possibility of this derivation, which was hypothesized by a great linguist, is being brought under consideration is the well-known close connection of Athene to pottery. A monument to this connection is the potter's song in the popular biography of Homer. The extraordinary significance of ceramics for prehistoric and historical Athens must be recognized, even if one is not inclined quite to label Athene a potters' Goddess on the basis of this etymology.[99] Pottery forms the precondition for metallurgy and thereby for bronze objects. Only in a later period was the festival of Chalkeia – named such after the material and art of the founders and smiths – celebrated exclusively by artisans as though it were a festival of Hephaistos.[100] Earlier it belonged among the most important festivals of Athene. The nine-month interval, during which the *peplos* for the Goddess (begun during Chalkeia) was completed, bound this festival to the festival of Panathenaia. The qualities of the Goddess as ruler of the city ("Polias") and as ruler of handicrafts ("Ergane") are bound up with one another additionally in many ways.[101]

It would be too much of a simplification, however, to assert that the *other* aspect hidden behind the martial Pallas and appearing in the name "Athene" is simply the protecting spirit of potters, founders, and smiths. From where, then, would have come the *feminine* image of this Deity? Would it not have been simpler to present her martial aspect as masculine, rather than as feminine and yet simultaneously masculine, as *virago*? It must be the case, then, that the image was created from a depth of artistic praxis where the divine forms are experienced directly and not cogitated. The polarity "Goddess of warriors" and "Goddess of artisans" does not express the complete self-contradiction of the image, in which both the *martial maiden* and the *protecting mother* are equally *patriarchally* defined, i.e., as feminine potentialities which serve the father, imitate him, and look after his interests in the next generation. It does express the characteristic feminine situation in a patriarchal order when Athene gets bound up with the God of masculine artisanship as Hephaistia, as the "Athene of Hephaistos" – like Athene Areia with Ares. Her statue occupied the second place in the temple of Hephaistos, the tutelary God of the Kerameikos, the potters' quarter.[102] In her own right, however, on the Acropolis, she protected and ruled over feminine handiwork, the weaving of wool, which in prehistoric times was also an epoch-making handicraft and as closely associated with the Athene religion as was bronze-casting or its predecessor, pottery-making.[103]

At one time this religion included and gave form to the whole of life. The possibility that one aspect of its supreme Goddess had to do with the production of one of the most important ancient arts of man must be admitted. An analogy to her name – if indeed "Athene" orginally meant a vessel – is preserved in Greek as well as in Roman religion. Like Hestia and Vesta, whose names refer to the hearth, Athene could also, according to her name, be associated with the hearth, as *eschara*, a fire container which in its portable form was a *coal pan*. The Goddess's sanctuary on the Athenian Acropolis, the Erechtheion,[104] which – comparable to the *aedes Vestae* in Rome – enclosed within itself so many of her mysteries, contained a fixed hearth of this sort. Granted, not even *one* aspect of the Goddess is fully explained without remainder in the *object*, or in the *concept*, of a fire vessel, as little as is the other aspect in the shield; yet an *image* of motherhood, of a golden core-concealing femininity, can be contained in the name "Athene" if it means the *vessel* of the sacred fire.

7

The duality of aspects appeared also in the attributes of certain cultic images of the Goddess. According to one description, even the Palladium, that ancient sacred image of Pallas which, as one version has it, fell from heaven,[105] already showed two aspects. In the right hand the statue carried a raised lance, in the left a distaff and spindle,[106] tools of feminine handiwork and of the household. It was not merely novel invention that attributed them to the mysterious statue; coins from Troy show us the statue equipped in this way in accordance with ancient tradition.[107] The statuette of an owl holding the distaff – a symbolic representation of the Goddess – has been preserved for us.[108] Of an archaic cultic image of Athene Nike it is attested that the simple statue held a pomegranate in the right hand and a helmet in the left.[109] The helmet undoubtedly refers to the "palladium" aspect. The pomegranate belongs to her as an attribute of mature womanhood. Even without reflecting on the mythological background, the meaning of this statue can be explicated: through it Athene is characterized as a guardian of human and vegetative fecundity.[110]

Yet precisely this symbolism has a solid mythological background. The symbol of the pomegranate belongs to Persephone, most likely since the pre-Greek period when the underworld Goddess was not yet associated with Demeter but with Rhea.[111] It is not only a fertility symbol, but points also to a specific aspect of the realm ruled over by the Great Mother Goddess Rhea: its underworldly aspect. Persephone ate some of the pomegranate, and since then she has belonged to Hades.[112] This has been classically understood as implying the fruit made her unfruitful. But, according to the understanding of all antiquity, she became the Queen of the realm of the dead. The pomegranate, with its internal richness of myriad kernels, is a miniature copy of the underworld's richness in souls, even of its fruitfulness if it is believed that souls of the living have come here from there or have returned here from there. Internal to this symbolism is the realm of death as the realm of souls.

The symbolic animal of Athene, the owl, was also related to the realm of the dead. According to one story, Askalaphos, the son of Acheron and Gergyra (which is a variant of Gorgon and thereby has a relation to Athene), was to blame for Persephone's enthrallment to Hades: he revealed that she had eaten part of the pomegranate, or he even seduced her into doing it. For punishment he was turned into a type of owl, which was called Askalaphos.[113] The similarity of the one aspect of Athene to Persephone is attested not only by the pomegranate and possibly also by the owl.

Festivals such as the Procharisteria or the Skira, which could be confused with festivals of Persephone,[114] can be merely mentioned as a further bit of evidence.[115] In her temple near the Boeotian town of Koroneia, Athene was worshipped together with Hades. Our source, Strabo, does not reveal the guarded secret of the mythologem which clarifies this association, but he does say explicitly that it came about "for some kind of mystical reason."[116] The Athenian in Plato's *Laws* names Athene frankly "our Kore and Despoina,"[117] or in other words "our Persephone."

Less certain is the duality of attributes in Athene as a city Goddess. It is present, however, at least on the vase painting[118] that shows the seated cultic image of Polias: beside her is the serpent, before her the priestess, the altar, and the steer being led to sacrifice. In her left hand she holds the helmet, in her right a bowl for catching the liquid sacrifice. It is a sacred vessel, without special reference to the art of pottery but perhaps with meaning in the Athene religion. It is striking how often since mythical and heroic times *bowls* are named in the lists of votive offerings brought to the Goddess in her famous cult in Lindos on Rhodes.[119] The bowl, in contrast to the helmet, characterizes the Goddess as recipient and thereby perhaps *more* her feminine side, *more* the "*Athene*" than the "Pallas."

8

Often the duality exists also in the number of chosen maidservants of the Goddess. On the oldest representation, the Mycenaean painted plate, one sees two devotees or priestesses. Nothing has been handed down regarding martial priestesses of Pallas, but we do know of two maidens who were designated for sacrifice and – provided they escaped – were consecrated to Athene. So it was with the two virgins who in archaic times were sent from Lokri to Troy as atonement for the crime which Aias had committed against the Palladium.[120] The Trojan men, meanwhile, waited and lay in ambush, and spying the maidens killed them, burned their corpses on the wood of barren trees – a feature which characterizes the dealing with sacrifices to Deities (presumably the Goddess) of the underworld – and scattered the ashes from Mount Traron into the sea. The Lokrians then had to send two other virgins to replace the ones sacrificed. If the Lokrian maidens remained unrecognized and reached the temple of Athene, they became priestesses of the Goddess. They kept the temple cleaned up, went about barefooted and wearing only one garment, and were allowed to do this only at night. Moreover, they were allowed neither to step in front of the Goddess nor to leave the temple. This second ordinance is not transmitted to us very clearly,[121] but the sacrifice of at least *one* virgin is credible. In an oriental Greek city, Laodikeia in Syria, Athene is supposed originally to have received the sacrifice of one virgin each year, later one doe.[122] In Salamis on Cyprus human sacrifices were offered to Aglauros, who shared a cult with Diomedes in the sanctuary of Athene.[123] Ephebes led the victim around an altar three times, and a priest impaled it with a lance. The corpse was cremated.

This example reveals something of the original meaning of human sacrifice to Pallas Athene. It seemingly belongs in continuity with those initiation rites through which young boys – and maidens, too, as brides –

were taken into patriarchal organizations. The oath of arms of the Athenian Ephebes was sworn, after all, in the sanctuary of Aglauros; among the Gods mentioned in the oath the war God appeared twice.[124] In the Cyprian cult, Diomedes substituted for Ares.[125] The shaven heads of the Lokrian virgins, who were priestesses of Athene, were characteristic of initiated boys and girls. The shaving off of hair belonged to the rites of initiation.[126] In accordance with the traditions mentioned above, it is probable that in completely archaic circumstances a male or female representative of the total group being initiated would be sacrificed, while for the others the shaved head signified having been sacrificed.[127] This barbaric-archaic practice took place only in a few locations and more toward the periphery of the Greek world. It provided the opportunity for stories such as the slaying of Pallas by Athene,[128] or the similar story of Iodama which will be mentioned shortly. The association of the Ephebes to Pallas became especially clear at one point: they accompanied a statue of the Goddess, appropriately called "Pallas" in the sources,[129] which for some reason was in need of cleaning, to the sea at Phaleron and after the washing back again to the city. In the mysterious happening through which "Pallas" became unclean, which has been kept completely secret, Aglauros most likely played the passive role.[130] One is able to get a glimpse only at the portion of the ceremony which occurred during the open procession of the statue; the darker, mystery enshrouded portion is more attached to specific maidenly figures.

One such maiden appeared in the Athenian story of Aglauros, who was a being in between the Great Goddess and one of her human servants. The cited festival of the washing of the cultic image – the Plynteria – was associated with her death.[131] One of the methods of slaying which is transmitted to us is turning the victim into stone,[132] for which the already mentioned fate of Iodama is the parallel. In the cult of Athene Itonia near Koroneia, which also has already been referred to because the Goddess shared a common worship with Hades there[133] ("for some mystical reason"),

Iodama played a role which again reminds us of the Lokrian virgins and their service. She was a priestess of Athene who entered the sanctuary at night. Once the Goddess appeared to her with the Gorgoneion on her breast, and at the sight of it she was turned to stone. For that reason a woman places *fire on the altar of Iodama* every day and calls out three times: "Iodama lives and wants fire!"[134] Athene Itonia, who turned the eternally living, fire-desiring Iodama into stone, is the Goddess of Alalkomena, the neighboring town to Koroneia, and as Alalkomenai she is a Pallas figure.[135] The wish of Iodama to have fire accords with the significance that she asks in the name of "Athene" as though it were her own,[136] and it shows also the difference between this Goddess and a "Hestia": fire does not glow eternally on the altar of Iodama but must be rekindled daily, just as is naturally the case with a coal pan, an *eschara*. The sanctuary lay on the river Koralios or Kuralios, presumably so named because the Goddess received the hair offerings of boys and girls there;[137] for this characteristic she bore the epithet Koria or Koresia.[138]

Aglauros and Iodama, the *sacrificed, slain, annihilated* – but nevertheless living – represent the *one* aspect of the Goddess that stands over against the other aspect called "Pandrosos" among the sisters of Aglauros but can also have the names "Pallas" or "Nike" or "Victory." Should Nike represent the Goddess, she could also be carrying the pomegranate and thereby imply the concealed other side. Neither of the two poles can exist without the other; always the two together, *in their opposition*, are Pallas Athene. It is not merely that a martial and a maternal existence are bound together and opposed to each other, but a *defensive* virginity, keeping at bay hostile aggression by the menace of death, and a virginity that falls *victim* to attack and death, whereby conception and motherhood come into being.

The fact that certain initiation rites in prehistoric times could involve the slaying of a virgin is relevant because this motif appears with remarkable frequency in Attic story as the voluntary or involuntary sacrifice of maidens for the sake of the king's victory, for the deliverance of the fatherland. Once it is the daughters of Erechtheus, three in number, of whom the father sacrifices one; the others go to their deaths voluntarily.[139] Or there are six of them so divided that two sacrifice themselves voluntarily and a group of four remains.[140] The victims possessed their death cult under the name "the virgins," a meaningful statement since such a cult could have its basis in the fact that virgins were once actually put to death. Among these may also be counted the four daughters of the Spartan Hyakinthos[141] whom the Athenians sacrificed and who were identified as the stars of the Hyades.[142] In the tale of the Athenian Leos – the first representative of the "people," which is what his name means, and also a priest of initiations who in this character was made into a son of Orpheus – there appear again three daughters who were sacrificed by their father.[143] Finally the death of Aglauros, in a leap from the stones of the Acropolis, was conceived as a voluntary death for the fatherland.[144] The fact that she was one of three sisters seems to have influenced the other tales.

9

Four Athenian maidens were chosen for the service of the Goddess and lived on the Acropolis. Between the ages of seven and eleven they were selected from among the noble families.[145] All were called Arrephoroi. Only two, however, are mentioned as executors of the secret rite of the Arrephoria.[146] It was also said in connection with the choice of the four Arrephoroi that two persons were chosen to direct the work on the *peplos* of the Goddess.[147] Not only maidens but also mature women helped in the weaving of it,[148] just as the priestess of Athene was herself not a virgin.[149] We do not know if the two directors of the work on the *peplos* were chosen from the four Arrephoroi. The question which concerns us relates only to the appropriateness of the four (or two) Arrephoroi on the one hand, and the three daughters of Kekrops, who functioned as examples for the conduct of the later Arrephoroi, on the other. The story was told to these girls when, at about the age of seven, they entered into the Arrephoria festival. Aglauros, one of three sisters, and a second sister as well, were killed because they opened the basket which the Arrephoroi carried and were not allowed to open. On Aglauros falls the shadow of Pallas Athene's darker aspect, the one bound up with the underworld. This shadow, however, was no longer an obvious factor for these small servants of the Goddess, all dressed in white and wearing golden ornaments. Only their number – two, or twice two – still implied the two aspects of their mistress. How are we to square this duality with the number of the three sisters?

In the midst of the serving girls belongs the priestess, the actual representative of the Goddess herself.[150] The function of this threesome is expressly declared:[151] the priestess of Polias has two assistants, one of them being called Trapezo ("she who brings the table") and the other Kosmo ("she who sets the table"). Of the three daughters of Kekrops, the middle one, Herse, comes to the fore less often than the first and third, Aglauros and Pandrosos.[152] Both of these are equated with the Goddess herself, the one as Athene Aglauros, the other as Athene Pandrosos.[153] Each possessed her own special sacred precinct: the Pandroseion lay up on the Acropolis, leaned directly against the Erechtheion, and surrounded the sacred olive tree; the Aglaureion lay below, on the north slope of the fortress. It was the place where Aglauros supposedly had jumped to, in self-sacrifice according to one version, out of insanity at having glimpsed the forbidden content of the basket according to another.[154] Herse shared the wrongdoing and the punishment with her, while Pandrosos remained the faithful servant of the Goddess. According to one less differentiated version, all three sisters were guilty.[155] Or it was Aglauros and Pandrosos who committed the sin of succumbing to curiosity.[156] Herse owned no particular sanctuary, yet the ceremony of the Arrephoria was associated with her name, or with what this name concealed within itself, by giving it a new interpretation or even by revising the name to Errephoria. She may be the figure in the middle who carries the essence of Athene – not so much one of her externally active *aspects* as her *mystery* – and for this reason had no other sanctuary than that in which the city Goddess was worshipped among mysterious cultic objects, i.e., the Erechtheion.

The cultic mysteries of the Erechtheion, which was the sacred precinct on which a unique building was constructed in classical times, are, as has been already mentioned, best compared to the mysteries of the vestal temples in Rome. Here, as there, we find the worship of a virginal and simultaneously maternal city Goddess.[157] Here, as there, we find virgins selected from among the most noble families to serve the Goddess: in this the Roman cult distinguishes itself by rigorous consistency, while the Athenian cult comes closer to a contradictory, more concrete reality through a seeming inconsistency – the divine *Virgin* has a mortal *married woman* for her priestess. Here, as there, we find associations to the elements:[158] to earth, represented on the Acropolis by the Goddess Ge; to water, which came into the Erechtheion from a bitter spring and was considered to be sea-water;[159] most importantly, however, to fire, which not only glowed in the *eschara* but also burned in an *eternal* lamp.[160] And finally, here, as there, we find the cultic presence of the masculine in unmistakeable forms: with Vesta it was the *fascinus*, the phallus, but in the sacred precinct of the Erechtheion, aside from the precisely analogous object which was a "Hermes"[161] covered with myrtle branches, a whole series of Gods and heroes expressed the same things in different, historically conditioned variations.

In the three sisters – Aglauros, Herse, and Pandrosos – and in the many forms of the divine "Man," who was the companion of the Goddess of the Erechtheion, we have the plan of a dramatically dynamic and yet firmly outlined mythologem, which plays itself out on several stages at the same time. The stage of the cult must be considered together with that of the mythological tales. The calendar of festivals leads over onto the cosmic stage, and yet we will move on it in a purely human way. Pallas Athene is on *all* stages, without fully revealing herself in any single appearance on this or that stage.

10

The myths and rites of the Athenian Acropolis, above all those associated with the Erechtheion, would teach us the most about Pallas Athene – precisely because they had no intention of instructing – could we but reconstruct them. But the cultic activities which guaranteed the existence of a city and the cultic objects with which these were carried out were kept no less secret than the *Arreta* of other, now famous mysteries. The myths that were told about these at once hint at the inexpressible and veil it. It is veiled through many devices: through numerous variations on the same theme, and through names that are nothing more than code-words. Intentionality and spontaneity are difficult to separate in this game, in which telling is combined with not surrendering.

Just as people of the south today switch into rapid dialect when they do not want strangers to understand them, the Athenians said Arrephoroi and Arrephoria instead of Arretophoroi and Arretophoria, [162] since even the word *arreton* ("unmentionable," "secret," "sacred," "horrible") betrayed more of what the maidens were carrying in the basket than was seemly for the service of the virginal Goddess. Playful variations, like Aglauros beside Agraulos (which has a more concrete meaning[163]) or Kekrops instead of Kerkops (a word in which the serpentine tail becomes too prominent), were supposed to deceive us. And they have actually deceived the educated people and romantic souls who have taken great pleasure in the "dew sisters." The name of the second sister, Herse, does indeed actually mean "dew," but dew can be a metaphor for fertilizing semen and also for the resulting child.[164] The masculine form of Herse would be a reference to Apollo and Zeus as divine children, who were given the epithets Hersos or Erros;[165] in its feminine form the name *intimates* the receptive one and at the same time *conceals* this. Who would have dared raise the veil had it not been for the fact that the fate of semen is spoken of explicitly in the wedding mythologem of Athene?[166] Pandrosos, too, seemingly had a *merely* poetic name ("the one completely bedewed" or "bedewing everything"), and here the bedewed olive tree and the moon, which dispenses dew,[167] become visible in a many-layered image. Wherever three mythological sisters appear, the cosmic background of the three lunar phases enters the picture, just as these played a part in Hera's three forms of manifestation.[168]

The calendar of Athene's festivals provides some further hints. The monthly birthday of the Goddess was always the third of the month, called Tritomenis, which through a false etymology was related to Athene's epithet, Tritogeneia.[169] During the festival of Panatheneae in the summer month of Hekatombaion, the birthday was celebrated in Athens as the new year. The Great Panathenaea was celebrated with great magnificence every fourth year. The most important day of the Panathenaea fell on the third day before the end of the month.[170] Accordingly, late antiquarians set the birthday on the third day before the end of the month,[171] or simply on the day of the hidden moon.[172] This mistaken but not completely groundless opinion can be explained: the day of the new moon, the *menōn phthinas 'emēra*, being the chief day of the festival,[173] received as much importance as did the actual birthday, which was the third day after the disappearance of the moon. The most important day of the Panathenaea and the birthday were associated but were not identical. The distance between them was not supposed to be greater than the time between the disappearance and reappearance of the moon. It became larger on the calendar, however, which preferred fixed numbers. The twenty-six to twenty-eight days during which the moon appears, along with the one-and-one-half to three days during which it does not appear, had to be extended in order to make up the *thirty* days of the calendar month.[174] The month could be extended either at the beginning or the end. If it were done at the beginning, the crescent of the new moon would appear on the evening of the month's third day. The birth of Athene actually remained connected to this day. If the month were extended at the end, the date of the moon's reappearance could occur as early as the twenty-ninth, i.e., the second day of the Panathenaea.[175] The festival could have begun previously, on the nights of the twenty-eighth, with the dancing, singing, and noise-making of the young men and women:[176] this is how the hidden moon was invoked in archaic times and by archaic peoples.[177] On the evening of the second day, the crescent of the new moon would become visible in the evening sky, as though having sprung from the head of the sun, a phenomenon in which we recognize the cosmic referent in the birth of Athene.[178] The greatest festival of Athene thus contained *two* cosmic situations: the time of the *conjunction*, the night of the new moon, which is shrouded in darkness and during which the sun and moon seemingly encounter one another, and an *epiphany*.

More than once already we have confronted among the aspects of the Goddess an image that reaches into the darkness. This is Aglauros, and like her two sisters, and in them Athene herself, she appeared on several stages at the same time. On the divine stage of *mythology* she occupied the periodic existence of a dying and eternally rising, immortal Goddess; on the human stage of *cultic legend*, she appeared as servant and priestess, the sacrificed and dying one. It is self-contradictory and yet suitable to the essence of this autonomous aspect of the Goddess that Euripides speaks of the three sisters sometimes as deceased and sometimes as alive, as dancing nymphs.[179] Pandrosos, like Pallas and Nike, is a name for the bright aspect, the aspect of epiphany. Aglauros, on the other hand, plays a tragic role in that mystery in which Pallas appears in need of purification.[180] There was express mention of mysteries of Aglauros and Pandrosos.[181] This does not refer to the Panathenaea, but to another festival in which the sinister side appeared in frankly tragic tones as the sacrificial death of a maiden, the festival of Plynteria.[182] The cleansing of Pallas belonged to this festival. The cleansing was completed toward the end of the month of Thargelion on a dark day during which all other activities were forbidden, an *apophras ēmera*[183] ("ominous day"). This was preceded by a brighter act, the Kallynteria,[184] which had to do with ornamenting the maiden who was supposed to enter into the darkness. This could only have been Aglauros, who by the ornamentation was characterized as a bride. "Agraulos," the original form of her name, means "the one spending the night in the field" and evokes the scenario of her Persephonian fate, which took place outside the fortress, presumably at the location of the Aglaureion. The playful transformation of the name – Aglauros probably not unintentionally harmonizes with the name of the Charity Aglaia[185] – elevates the image into a higher sphere, while that original nocturnal scenario in the field reminds us also of the fate of the Lokrian maidens[186] for whom the men of Troy lay in ambush with murderous intentions. But to whom did Agraulos fall?

The masculine is related to this aspect of Athene in two historically consecutive manifestations. Sophocles alludes to the oldest of the masculine partners when, imitating the form of the name "Agraulos," he gives the three sisters, or one of them, the epithet *drakaulos*.[187] The explanations for this are varied: it was because Athene allowed the serpent to live with her; or, because she lived with the double-formed Kekrops; or, because one of the sisters used to spend nights with the serpent of the Acropolis and days with the Goddess.[188] Translated into the language of saga, this relationship was spoken of as follows: Agraulos became the wife of Kekrops and the mother of Kekrops' daughters, who were then also called the daughters of Agraulos.[189] She is associated to Kekrops in *two* ways: as *daughter* and as *spouse.* The dual relationship was corrected in a pseudo-historical geneology, where the spouse of Kekrops was given another father, one who had been especially invented for her.[190] Another tale of incest comes to the fore in connection with the name Aglauros. According to this story, Prokris, a daughter of Erechtheus, bore a child named Aglauros *to her own father.*[191] The third instance of it comes up in the birth mythologem of Athene herself, since *she herself* possessed the characteristics, under the name of Metis, of a wife of Zeus. The fourth instance of the same is connected to Gorge, who bore Tydeus to her father Oineus.[192] Athene, to whom the name Gorge refers as much as does Gorgyra in the stories about Askalaphos,[193] then became the maternal Protectress as much of Tydeus as of his son Diomedes, whom we come upon in an obscure cultic connection with Aglauros on Cyprus. Pallas provides the fifth instance, who as father waylays his own daughter Pallas, even if the act of incest does not succeed in the diluted form of this mythologem.[194] It is to the *father*, then, that the *daughter* falls victim in this mythic region – at least in the stories, though not in the cult. He allows her to descend into the darkness. And it is the daughter who offers the sacrifice: *she* descends into a paternal-masculine darkness. When the last crescent disappears before the approach of the first fully moonless night, it is the situation of the vanished Metis. The strange image of the devoured wife of Zeus also corresponds to a purely human situation: the binding of the daughter to the father, out of which the patriarchal family order, as opposed to the matriarchal, could most easily arise. The darkness here is just as little purely cosmic – i.e., mythologically and cultically bound up with the time of the dark moon – as it is when Persephone is seized. That to which one succumbs and falls defenselessly always has a lethal aspect, the more so here where the masculine appears not *graciously* and paternally but *aggressively*, like the father in the father-daughter mythologem. This mythologem lies at the foundation of the Athene religion.

11

In the second form whereby the masculine determines the fate of Aglauros, the aggressive element comes even more into the foreground and with it too an institution which, one must believe, introduced the formation of the patriarchal family. The presupposition for this development was the father-daughter mythologem, which is the mythological correlate to that mutual alliance that can exist with such uncanny force between father and daughter. To put it in more general terms, it is the bondedness of the feminine portion of humanity, and of the feminine part of each individual person, *to the paternal origin*. Over against this stands the mother-son mythologem, which is the mythological correlate to the alliance between mother and son; or, the bondedness of the masculine portion of humanity, and of each individual, to the maternal origin. This is the basis of every kind of matriarchal organization. Both mythologems are in themselves timeless. As tales of actual incest they make an *archaic* impression. They may both be present at the same time, at the same time too with the mother-daughter and father-son mythologems, which are two *identity-mythologems*, while the former are *conjunction-mythologems*. The chronological sequence of the mother-son mythologem as the older, followed by the father-daughter mythologem as the more recent, and the passage from the first over into the second, would be easy to grasp psychologically. It would also be easy to call the basic mythologems *archetypal*. Nevertheless, the stages of the process, and even the direction of it, are phenomena which the historian of cultures and religions must decipher from concrete prehistoric and historical materials, if he wishes to present more than a purely theoretical construction. The institution of young men's initiations, which forms the transitional stage between social organization based on mother-right to that based on father-right, will not be invented here; rather it will be reconstructed on the basis of materials handed down to us. Here we are standing on ground where a relative chronology is possible.

The image of Athene is conditioned by bondedness to the father. She has the contradictory task of providing progeny for the father while yet remaining the father's daughter and refraining from completing herself with a man, unlike Hera, whose history with Zeus presents another conjunction-mythologem, that of brother-and-sister. Ares, who enters into a relationship with Aglauros, is hardly to be conceived of as theriomorphic in this connection, but rather as the mythological model and representative of those young men who swore an oath of arms in the Aglaureion and became thereby bearers and defenders of the patriarchal order. The God of warfare himself appears as father and defender of the same order, not as father and husband of his own daughter, however, but rather as the model of the earthly father because he kills the attacker of his daughter, Halirrothios, son of Poseidon. For this he is called by Poseidon before a divine tribunal of justice on the Areopagus.[195] The name of the daughter whom Aglauros bore to him, Alkippe, and the name of the attacker, Halirrothios, denote the last period in the formation of the Athene religion and mythology as *Athenian* religion and mythology. This period stimulated no change in the fundamental mythologem of the fortress's sanctuaries, no transformation of the father-daughter mythologem. This had been the mythologem of the fortress Goddess at least since Mycenaean times and so it remained, stated or half-stated. There did occur, however, a representative happening, stimulated not by a father but by an aggressive son, and soon thereafter a new animal appeared on the scene. A new wave of theriomorphism entered with the image of the *horse*, an animal which had been associated with the Goddess already earlier outside of Athens. In Athens the hippomorphic elements that were taken up, after the anthropomorphic association with Ares had been made, meant a cultural regression, and this probably occurred in the post-Mycenaean period.

Alkippe, "the courageous mare," or "the courageous, like a mare," was an aspect of Athene just as was her mother Aglauros, who for her part was the double of her mother, the wife of Kekrops. With Alkippe, the role of aggressor was taken by Halirrothios, the son of Poseidon. According to his name ("he who storms with the sea"), he can be none other than Poseidon himself, who, of all the Greek Gods, was most closely associated with the horse. Precisely this name, however, reveals a connection which is more recent in the stories about Poseidon than is his association with the horse. In Greek mythology the image of Poseidon as "Lord of the Sea" is a more recent manifestation of this God than is his role as husband of the Earth Goddess and Lord of the Mainland.[196] It was in this original character that he put forward the horse as his offer in the story of his competition with Athene for possession of the land of Attica.[197] The denouement of the competition was that Poseidon stayed outside the Acropolis and its cults; there, the militant Pallas, who had come there from the northern territories, was recognized and accepted for her essential relatedness to the Mycenaean fortress Goddess, though without the hippomorphic accompaniment. Only later was Poseidon associated with the salty spring on the Acropolis in his character as sea God. What is decisive for the chronology, aside from the narrative accounts which tell of the defeat of Poseidon, is the topography. The place where the God presented the steed – his semen fell on the rocks,[198] which seems to be an echo of the story about Hephaistos and Athene – and where he was worshipped as Hippios, together with Athene Hippia, was the rocky hill *Kolonos.*[199] (Outside of Athens, in Olympia, Athene – as Athene Hippia – is even connected hippomorphically with Ares, as Ares Hippios.[200]) The places of association with Ares, too, lay in the *outer* regions, located around the Acropolis to the north and west. Kolonos lay out in an even more distant place.

The chronological inference which one can draw from the topography is confirmed by the geneological line of descent: Kekrops and Aglauros represent the first generation; Ares and Aglauros, daughter of Aglauros, form the second; Halirrothios (son of Poseidon) and Alkippe make up the third. Finally, the same inference is to be drawn from the fact that the mythologem of the sacred wedding of the Goddess with a hippomorphic God never became official but remained a private tradition.[201] It was never forgotten that originally there had been a wedding,[202] but the story was more familiar in another form: in the family of Kodros it happened that Hippomenes, one of the Kodrians, surprised his daughter while she was with a man; he bound the seducer to a chariot and then locked his daughter in a building with a horse, which was afterwards referred to as the deserted sanctuary of "the horse and the maiden."[203] The hippomorphic parallel to the wedding of the Athenian "Queen" with Dionysos, the *bull God*, should not be overlooked. The name Leimone ("she of the meadow") indicates the original place of the wedding as being somewhere outside the city. In Athens the hippomorphic setting of the mythologem, which had earlier been associated with the serpent and bull, remained on the *periphery*. The horse belongs to the latest level of the Athenian religion and mythology of Pallas Athene. The hippomorphic elements are just as late as another element which most probably came with it: the Gorgon's head.[204] Mounted on the shield or the aegis – the sacred goatskin which was an even more archaic cultic requisite of the Goddess – it only increased the terrors which one admits were a part of the Agraulos cult and its associated initiations.

12

The scenes of the attacks on Agraulos and Alkippe lay outside the fortress, one on the north slope, the other on the south slope; meanwhile the serpent had its home and Kekrops his grave on the Acropolis, in the sacred location which was named after Erechtheus. The Erechtheion included other manifestations of the masculine as well.[205] In front of the entrance stood an altar to Zeus Hypatos. In the west wall of the building, which differed from the standard type of Greek temple, was an altar to Poseidon, on which were offered sacrifices to Erechtheus as well. Further in, there was an altar to the hero Butes, and finally a third altar, to Hephaistos. One of the chambers contained a wooden Hermes (i.e., a wooden phallus) which was concealed among myrtle branches and considered to be a votive offering of Kekrops. This would have been a middle area of the temple, since Herse, the beloved of Hermes, according to the story of their *hieros gamos*, lived in the middle room.[206] Except for the oldest fixed cultic image of the Goddess, everything in the contained temple – beginning with the three depressions in the north hall which were supposedly traces of Poseidon's trident[207] – was meant to remind one of the power and presence of masculine Deities. A salty spring (the "sea water") in the Erechtheion did not count as a feminine element like the earth, but as the "sea of Erechtheus"[208] also signified a masculine presence. This name identifies Erechtheus with the sea God Poseidon: indeed, he possessed a common cult with Poseidon and was associated with him as well through the double name Poseidon Erechtheus.[209] On the other hand, his being earth-born and the foster-child of Athene[210] associates him with Erichthonios. Judged by its ending,[211] the name Erechtheus is older than the combination Eri-chthonios, this latter name being a playful interpretation of the first. Concealment seems to be the main intention here, and this signified a secret: namely, that the *husband* and the *son* of the motherly

Goddess were identical, a theme that fits in with the mother-son mythologem.[212]

On the basis of what has been presented, it is possible to establish a relative chronology among the recounted forms of the masculine. Kekrops and the serpent – basically the *same* divine Person – and Erechtheus-Erechthonios (the son-husband) belong to the oldest level; Poseidon belongs to the most recent. In no sense at all did Ares intrude into the series of the fortress's masculine Deities: the cult outside the fortress's sanctuaries was suited to his nature, though he was in the vicinity of the fortress before Poseidon was. The close connection inherent in the name "Poseidon Erechtheus" associates an earlier spouse with the latest intruder. Over against this final result of a long development there are three manifestations of the masculine which remained independent, all of which are more archaic than Poseidon: Butes, whose name implies the period of the bull; Hephaistos, a pre-Greek God;[213] and "Hermes," an archaic cultic token. The epithet Zeus Hypatos may also indicate that he belonged to the most recent level, although he could also have been already present alongside the dark serpent, bull, and stallion husbands as the bright aspect of father. A bull spouse is presupposed by the hero Butes, not in the person of a "cattle-herd" – which is what his name means – but as an actual bull. We should say something about this before considering the relationship of the Goddess to her most obvíous masculine partner, Hephaistos.

13

To understand why the hero Butes had his cult in the Erechtheion it would be sufficient to know that he was honored as the founding ancestor of the family which served as priestesses of Athene and as priests of the God associated with her, i.e., Poseidon Erechtheus in historical times. He was the ancestor of the Butadai, or more strongly accentuated, of the Eteobutadai, the "true Butadai."[214] Besides this it is noteworthy that Butes, whom the old genealogies made into a son of Poseidon,[215] expresses a special relationship to cattle. Most likely it was the same relationship as the one which necessitated the very ancient and intricately executed cattle offerings to Zeus Polieus, which was also a name in the fortress for the masculine partner of Athene Polias. This relationship was certainly different from that to plow oxen, which was represented in the area of Pallas Athene's cult by *another* hero, Buzyges, the "cattle yoker," and by another family, the Buzygai. The Buzygai undertook the sacred plowing at the foot of the Acropolis, which occurred third in a series of sacred plowings of the Athenians.[216] The two different heroes, Butes and Buzyges, describe two stages within the Athene cult of the domestication of cattle. In the earlier stage, cattle were sacred and not yet used to do work, but they were killed in certain festivals. Several families took part in the sacred slaughtering of the bull on the Acropolis, among them the Kentriadai, which is indicated by their name ("the goaders").[217] They probably represent a rudiment of prehistoric bull-fighting as it was practiced in Crete.

The origin of the sacred slaughtering of the bull certainly lies in the old-Mediterranean level of Greek religion and could well be Minoan. In contrast, the Buzygai were the bearers not only of a later stage of domestication – yoking cattle and plowing with them – but also of a relatively new orientation: they would allow no cattle whatsoever to be killed.[218] This attitude may have played a part in the formulation of the bull-killing on the Acropolis – the Buphonia. The slaughtering of the bull belongs to the period *before* the second stage of full domestication, before the Buzygian stage. The hero Butes cannot be either contemporary with or later than the hero Buzyges: one must place him and the bull in an older period of the Athene cult. Athene received cattle offerings on the Acropolis no less frequently than Zeus Polieus, and she received them in the aspect which was different from the bright Pandrosos. After one had offered a *cow*, one had to sacrifice a *sheep* to Pandrosos.[219] If Erechtheus and Zeus were celebrated with cattle offerings,[220] it was also true that the Goddess in her dark aspect belonged to a divine partner who had *the form of a bull*. It is not without reason that she shares the epithet Hellotis, which she bears in Marathon and Corinth, with Europa, the bride of Zeus, whom he abducted after he had taken the form of a bull.[221] And it is certainly no accident that a black-figured Attic vase shows Athene on one side and the "Goddess on the bull"[222] on the other. The recognized function of Athene's servants Trapezo and Kosmo[223] can be connected to the receiving of the sacred bull, which preceded the Buphonia, the sacrifice of the bull to Zeus Polieus. The slaughterer of the bull, too, was among the servants of the Goddess. Among the names which are handed down for the first killer of the bull, Diomos is a short form of Diomedes, as that favorite hero of Athene, cultic comrade of Aglauros, and double of Ares was otherwise called.[224] It seems to have been a self-contradictory cultic drama in which the Goddess confronted the bull-formed one: she was ambivalently bound to him.

14

Easier to sketch are the outlines of the Goddess's relationship with Hephaistos, the masculine principle in the image of fire. The fire God not only had his altar in the Erechtheion but was present there in the eternally burning lamp which, like the fire of Vesta in Rome, had to be cared for by a priestess. The difference between these two cults – the priestess of Athene was not a virgin but a married woman – is small in comparison to the similarity of their relationship to fire. In Rome, as has already been pointed out, this relationship was more abstract than it was in Athens.[225] The cultic legend of Athene Hellotis in Corinth gives us an idea of the original concreteness of this fire worship. This legend comes down to us in a somewhat confused form,[226] but it shows a remarkable correspondence to the fate of the Lokrian maidens who were sacrificed to Athene and then cremated. Sometimes two sisters are mentioned, sometimes four. Among their names are Hellotis (an epithet of both Athene and Europa), Eurytione (a parallel form to Europa), and Chryse (also a name for Athene).[227] According to one version, a distressed Hellotis takes her younger sister Chryse with her into the temple of Athene and throws herself into the fire. According to the other version, the two sisters Hellotis and Eurytione, together with a child, died in the fire of Athene's temple, and the festival of Hellotia was used as an atonement for their deaths by fire. The succumbing of a virgin who represented the Goddess, or even of two virgins who corresponded to her two aspects, to the God of fire is demonstrated in this material.

In a series of cultic artifacts and mythological traditions, another aspect of Hephaistos' relationship to Athene comes to the fore: here he is not the consuming God of fire, but the bridegroom, husband, and father of a divine child. In the month of Pyanopsion the festival of Apaturia was celebrated, at which the youth of Athens, in phratries ("brotherhoods") and under the protection of Zeus Phratrios and Athene Phratria, received the initiation which they needed in order to get married. It was a kind of maturational ceremony.[228] At this festival Hephaistos was particularly celebrated: men, dressed in their most beautiful garments, lit the torch at the fire of the hearth, sang in praise of their God, and sacrified to him.[229] There is no report in the fragmentary evidence of a torchlight procession, but such can safely be assumed, and for the Corinthian Hellotia a report of such is handed down explicitly. On the last day of the same month began the festival which Hephaistos and Athene shared in common, the Chalkeia. The secret of this festival was not given away, with the result that more stories were told about it, such as that Athene was given to Hephaistos and placed in a chamber for him, or that he followed her and embraced her.[230] All variations allow the Goddess to leave the embrace a virgin, but they also allow a *child* to originate from this same embrace, born from the semen of the God which was received by the earth, and then handed over to Athene. According to one version the sacred *wool* of the Goddess with which the divine semen was caught also played a role in the story.[231]

Marriage, pregnancy, and victorious maidenhood are the given elements, and the self-contradictory relations among them is what the various stories seek to explain. A cultic epithet of the Goddess seems to refer to the same episode, which was related in so many variations and yet to a certain extent was kept secret. In Sparta, Athene was called Chalkioikos ("she of the bronze chamber"), and supposedly she owned a temple there made of bronze.[232] Of what else could the wedding chamber have been made in which the smith God Hephaistos locked himself with her? Greek mythology also knows of a bronze wedding chamber in which the bridegroom appeared not as fire but as golden rain. This occurs in the story of Danaë, the mother of Perseus, a hero who was a special protégé of Athene.[233] This is also, however, a motif in the mythology of Athene: according to a tradition on Rhodes, Zeus permitted golden rain to fall when the Goddess sprang from his head.[234] Gold is also associated with a divine child in the religion of Athene, and the simultaneity of the birth of *this child* and the birth of *the Goddess herself* belongs to the mysteries of this religion. We turn now to the child. His birth owes to the association of the Goddess with the fire God, even though it is the Earth Goddess, a cultic companion of Athene on the Acropolis,[235] who appears as the pregnant one in the camouflaged stories.

15

The name Erichthonios (the "very chthonic one"), a playful interpretation of the name Erechtheus, and used in further playful interpretations,[236] remained the name of the mysterious child. It would perhaps be incorrect to say that this added the aspect "son" to the earlier aspects of the masculine partner of the Goddess, i.e., "father" and "husband." The reason for this is that in the mother-son mythologem, which preceded the father-daughter mythologem also on the Acropolis of Athens, the "son" became the husband: the father was in no way yet present at the beginning of a divine genealogy that began with the mother. Without father or brother, virginity would have been meaningless, since it is a form of the most intimate connection with either one or the other of them, even when it appears as absolute independence. At some point the third aspect, "father," was added to "son" and "husband," and at this same moment the aspect "maiden" was added to "mother" and "wife." From that moment on Pallas Athene was present.

Present as well was the son, who was always called by the pseudonym Erichthonios. There was a secret tradition concerning him, which Aristotle exposed[237] and later systematizers of Greek mythology after him retained. According to this, Athene is explicitly assigned a son by Hephaistos with the name Apollo, and the two of them are described as protective Deities (*tutela* and *custos*) of the city of Athens.[238] An inscription in the vicinity of the city celebrates Apollo with the epithet Hersos, which associates him (as divine child) with the Erechtheion.[239] If the reading of "Lethe" in a passage by Plutarch is correct,[240] then there stood in this same sanctuary an altar to the recognized mother of Apollo, who instead of openly being named Leto was hidden behind a playful pseudonym.[241]

Shining through all this mystery is a "sun child," neither more nor less sunlike than Apollo himself on Delos.[242] The Athenians decorated and handled their newly born children in accordance with this example. When they gave the infants a serpentine golden necklace and placed them in round baskets, as Euripides tells of Ion (the son of Apollo and Kreusa, daughter of

Erechtheus), the practice represented a repetition of what happened to the divine child on the Acropolis.[243] That child was guarded by serpents, but it was also represented as having the form of a serpent or serpentine feet.[244] The color of gold, suited to a sun child, also has a mythological meaning, which comes to light in various remarks that have come down to us. Aglauros loves gold, and Hermes can bribe her with gold to let him in to see Herse.[245] The serpent of the Acropolis, too, is supposed to have been especially fond of gold, and for this reason the Athenians wore their characteristic golden hair ornaments.[246] But the golden ornamentation became sacred only after the servants of the Goddess, the Arrephoroi, put them on.[247] It was these same Arrephoroi, who, imitating the daughters of Kekrops but less curious than they, carried the basket with the unknown contents out of the fortress into a sanctuary on the north slope of the Acropolis. Supposedly neither they nor the priestess herself to whom they turned over the basket knew what it contained or what they brought back as they returned to that other sanctuary on the Acropolis. But the rite becomes intelligible through the story which the Arrephoroi were told to keep them from opening the basket.

As one of the disguised stories tells it,[248] Athene wanted to feed the child secretly whom she had taken from the Earth Mother, to make it immortal. She turned the infant over to Aglauros and her sisters in a locked basket with the strictest prohibition: they must not know and must not investigate what the basket concealed. This would be understandable if the child was Athene's, a child no less mysterious than the Underworld Goddess's child whose birth was celebrated at Eleusis. This placing of the child under lock and key would not be understandable, however, if it had actually to do only with its *nourishment*. The Arrephoroi had to do something similar to what the daughters of Kekrops did: before the great festival they had to remove something from the fortress which corresponded to the newly born divine child. The time of their doing this is given by Pausanias as the night before the "festival."[249] No one would think of any other festival than the Panathenaea had the month of Skirophorion not been stated explicitly for it.[250] This was the month of the great bull sacrifice and the "mysteries" preceding it,[251] i.e., the festival of Skira, in which the priestess of Pallas Athene the priest of Poseidon Erechtheus, and the priest of Helios all participated.[252] That a secret unmentionable object (*Arreta*) was carried in a sealed basket in rites held outside the fortress also at this festival cannot be doubted. During the night before the Panathenaea, however, there took place a mysterious basket-carrying (an *Arrephoria*) also, and probably this one was distinguished from the other by naming it with the playful variation Hersephoria.[253]

A natural calculation sets aside any doubt about the *meaning* of the basket-carrying during the night preceding the Panathenaea. Athene and Hephaistos were celebrated together at the festival of Chalkeia, earlier called *Athenaia*. This day, the last day of the month of Pyanopsion, was celebrated like a wedding: the artisans presented grain swingles to the Goddess.[254] It was the custom to carry these about at Attic weddings, and they would otherwise actually have been out of place here.[255] Nine months after this wedding celebration, the Panathenaea (also earlier called the Athenaia) was celebrated. This nine-month interval, about which we earlier knew only that it served the purpose of weaving a new *peplos* for the Goddess, now becomes intelligible. Before the birth of Athene as virginal daughter of her father is celebrated in the fortress, two servants leave with a locked basket. On the basis of new excavations, their path can be traced precisely:[256] they left the Acropolis via an underground stairway which led northwest into the Aglaureion. The maidens, however, had to bend from this path eastward, and there they came upon the grotto sanctuary. According to Pausanias, their goal was supposed to be the sacred precinct of "Aphrodite in the Garden." Whether this name should be attributed to the grotto sanctuary remains an open question. The cavern was a sanctuary of

Aphrodite and Eros and full of cultic monuments to both of these Deities, among them stone phalluses and representations of the divine child Eros. After the maidens had returned to the sanctuary of the Virgin Athene, carrying another and again mysterious burden, they were removed from service and others were chosen to replace them.

On the basis of everything we have presented here, we must assume that the basket contained symbolic objects which, at least on the way down, signified the divine child. It has actually been handed down that the *Arreta* of the basket were serpents and male members made of dough.[257] Whether distinct objects are meant here or a single form, made of cake, that united them and could be conceived of in this way or that, remains beyond our current knowledge. Perhaps on the way down it was a serpent figure; it was said explicitly that Athene had given birth to a serpent[258] and that Erichthonios was a serpent,[259] and the form of a serpent was also not incompatible with the name of Apollo, who could as well appear as divine serpent.[260] On the way back up, the basket could hold differently shaped cakes, i.e., those of which it was said that they had been baked for the basket-carrying maidens, for the Arrephoroi:[261] the *anastatoi*, whose name indicates a phallic shape. Perhaps the servants were given these when they were removed from service after the festival, having been initiated into future motherhood through the mysteries which they carried.

The removal of the divine child prepared things for the second phase of the festival, i.e., the rebirth of the Goddess in victorious virginity as Pandrosos, Pallas, and Nike. The human analogy is not easy to find for this rapid sequence of *motherhood* followed by *rebirth as maiden*, which is the most peculiar paradox of Athene's nature. Even if every woman and every soul has something irreducibly virginal within, which is restored after every pregnancy and period of fruitfulness, this still does not occur as an epiphany immediately following the birth of the child. Here we must observe not only the *human*, but also the *cosmic*, time-frame. In the familiar Attic calendar, the Panathenaea follows the Chalkeia by an interval of nine thirty-day months. The human period of pregnancy may be mirrored in this. But if the months all contained thirty days, the two festivals could not possibly occur during the same phase of the moon. In *this* calendar the agreement is only approximate. In the same month of Pyanopsion, whose last day was the day of the Chalkeia, there occurred a festival which was supposed to prepare for the wedding celebration of Athene and Hephaistos, the Apaturia. At the Apaturia the marriageable young men sang the praises of the fire God.[262] The moment of conception, i.e., the festival that would correspond to the Christian celebration of the Annunciation, and that (as we shall soon see) had a significance only on the human, not on the cosmic, level, had to follow soon after, even if it was not a new-moon festival. The character of the Panathenaea as new-moon festival and as preparation for the birth of Pallas Athene allows the conclusion that there was a correspondence between the mythological transformation of the Goddess and the transformation of the moon. But one has to consider this cosmic transformation from the standpoint which is yielded from the *essence* of the Goddess Pallas Athene.

With Hera the correspondence of the mythological and cosmic transformations extended to all of the three phases in which the Greeks saw the moon: she corresponded to the waxing moon as maiden, to the full moon as fulfilled wife, to the waning moon as abandoned, withdrawing woman. The phase which showed Hera's essence in its fullest development was the full moon. From the viewpoint of Athene, the most essential phase is the exact opposite, the darkest night preceding her birth. Corresponding to her essence is the blackest darkness in which only the eyes of the owl can grasp the hidden light, wherein from the conjunction of the sun and moon *both* luminaries once more proceed forth: first the sun, a divine child, then the new moon, the virgin. On the cosmic stage, birth follows conjunction immediately, without pregnancy. Now in the heavens the Goddess is manifested as bright and virginal, again shining after the dark period like a winged Nike or a martial Pallas and recognizable by the shield. Thus we can understand the assertion of the ancients, attributed to Aristotle himself[263] and repeatedly stated: Pallas Athene is the moon,[264] although she is much *more* than only the moon.

The humanly impossible, rapid change out of dark motherhood into bright virginity is discernible against the cosmic background. The inner tension and opposition between *motherhood* and a maidenhood that is dedicated to the father and signifies a prohibition against all other men is a human reality. If we have understood the peculiar birth of Pallas Athene through the epiphany of the new moon, we must not forget the bondedness of a real father's daughter to her progenitor, to the dominant *spirit of the father*. The incestuous character of this bond is explicit only in archaic mythologems and stories and in collective dreams, phenomena which fall outside of that order which the Greeks called Themis.[265] Within this order the same bond became the foundational pillar of the patriarchal family. The father's daughter among the Gods stands beside the sons of the father, delivering over to the young men the maidens so that they will become *mothers*, but the lordship of the *paternal spirit* perdures above everything else.

Appendix

ON THE GOATSKIN AND THE GORGONEION

It has been more than fifty years since Sir William Ridgeway, in a meeting of the Cambridge branch of the Hellenic Society, presented the thesis that the aegis and the Gorgoneion [Gorgon-head or -mask] of Pallas Athene were originally one *single goatskin*, and therefore basically the same dress as was worn by the inhabitants of the Aegian region in primitive times. In the case of the aegis, however, an opening was cut behind the animal's head so that it hung down on the breast of the wearer; either the edges of the skin were cut into fringes, or leather fringes were sewn on. The pendulous animal head was especially elaborated and decorated, until finally it looked like what Homer described: the Gorgon-head of a fearsome monster (*Gorgeiā kephalā deinoio pelōrou*). A brief report of the meeting adds: "A Dyak's skin-costume, trimmed with feathers and embellished with a plate of shell where the head should be, was exhibited in support of the argument."[266]

This illustration was not badly chosen, since shortly thereafter a whole series of remarkable parallels to the religious practices of the ancient Mediterranean region (mostly Italian, however) was discovered among the tribes of Borneo, which are referred to collectively by the name "Dyak" or "Dayak."[267] Also worthy of mention is the recently accepted custom there of substitutionary animal sacrifice in place of human sacrifice.[268] It would be appropriate at this point, too, to test and evaluate these parallels using the methods recently employed on the parallels between West Ceramician (therefore also Indonesian) myths and rites and Greek ones.[269]

But the question of the identity between aegis and Gorgoneion is also raised by the interpretation of a classical text. The attempt here[270] is to come closer to a solution of this problem on the basis of enlarged and methodologically more strictly handled antique materials.

In the report mentioned above, no textual reference is cited in support of the identity of aegis and Gorgoneion. Repeating his theses,[271] Ridgeway appealed only to Herodotus, IV, 189: this passage maintains that the Greeks borrowed the dress and the aegis of their Athene statues from the Libyans, with the difference that the Libyans were dressed in goats' leather completely, with a red-colored goatskin as cloak, and that the fringes of the cloak were of leather and not of serpents. From this follows nothing that has to do with its identity with the Gorgoneion. The etymolologically unobjectionable and securely proven fundamental meaning of the aegis as goatskin – one sees the dangling goat's head and feet also in an Etruscan representation[272] – is corroborated by Herodotus. Moreover, the serpent-fringes appear on images of an aegis-bearing Athene which show no trace of the Gorgoneion or of the shield with the Gorgoneion drawn on it. The serpents form a special element that could be combined either with the aegis or with the Gorgoneion. One can agree with Ridgeway if he wishes to conceive of the original aegis without the traditional serpentine perimeter. Whether he is also correct in his repeated emphasis that it was a common costume which had no sacred or, as he expresses it, secret significance, is another question and one which will occupy us further.

First of all we must refer to the text which contains the problem of the identity between aegis and Gorgoneion, a text which already for F. A. Paley was "a *locus classicus* on the aegis of Pallas."[273] It is a passage from Euriphides' *Ion.* Creusa and the old man are speaking (lines 989 - 993):

Creusa: Earth there produced an awful monster, Gorgon.

Old Man: To harass all the gods and help her children?

Creusa: Yes, but destroyed by Zeus's daughter Pallas.

Old Man: Is this the tale which I have heard before?

Creusa: Yes, that she wears its skin upon her breast.

Old Man: Athene's armor which they call her aegis?

Creusa: So called from how she rushes into the battle.

Old Man: What was the form of this barbaric thing?

Creusa: A breastplate armed with serpent coils.

The meaning of this somewhat formal, dialogical statement is that the aegis of Pallas Athene, a breastplate with serpentine border, was originally the head or the hide of the Gorgon and her natural defense before the Goddess overcame and beheaded her. It was no invention of Euripides but rather – as line 994 makes apparent [274] – an old tradition which the poet, perhaps through a wordplay – as if *aegis* had come from *aizen* ("So called from how she rushed into battle") [275] – could powerfully combine with the fact that the easily removable breastplate which the priestess of Athene wore on certain occasions [276] was called "Aegis," i.e., goatskin. If the aegis had not been decorated with the Gorgoneion, this story could never have been told. But there is another tradition which distinguishes itself from the one which became classical through Hesiod's *Theogony* (line 280), by maintaining that the Gorgon was *skinned* rather than *beheaded* (*tās d'ote dā Perseus kephalān apedeirotomāsen*). There can be no doubt that the beheading was original to the Gorgon mythologem. Already in Homer the Gorgon's head appears by itself.[277] If in Athens a hide (*deros*), the result of flaying, was talked about, or if such a story could even have been accepted, there must have been a reason for it which was stronger than the perception of the Gorgon's head on the breast of the Goddess, etched into the aegis. This head could be removed and even stolen: it was lost during the flight from the Persians and was later stolen several times.[278]

The existence of this second motif, the motif of skinning, in the cultic sphere of Pallas Athene is demonstrated by the most infrequent stories. They contradict the Homeric religion and the whole classical tradition so decisively that they cannot be rejected as groundless. They must rest on archaic elements of the Athene religion that have been transmitted to us only through accidental utterances. According to one such utterance, the Pallas statue of Troy was dressed in "the skin of a man" (*andros dora*).[279] According to one description of the war against the Giants, it was the Giant Pallas whose skin Pallas Athene pulled off and used as a shield.[280] In another source, this same Pallas appeared with wings on his ankles,[281] or otherwise winged,[282] and was considered to be the father of Athene who had ambushed his daughter and was therefore so gruesomely treated by her.[283] As an archaic winged being, this Giant and father Pallas was similar to the Gorgon,[284] who according to Euripides' *Ion* (line 988) was overcome by the Goddess in the war against the Giants. According to another version, however, the conquered monster was supposed to resemble an animal. Indeed, it was a fire-spitting animal with the name of Aegis, whose pelt Pallas Athene afterwards wore as a breastplate.[285]

In all these tales the same motif is played in different variations: the flaying of a monster who, according to the characteristics of the Giant Pallas, must be judged to have been a *masculine* and *lascivious* creature. Neither the flaying nor these qualities fit the Gorgon, but they do fit the fundamenta meaning of the aegis as goatskin. It is, however, by no means self-evident that Athene wore the pelt of this animal as a customary primitive dress, as Ridgeway would have it, nor as the oldest protective device for battle, as the contemporary conception maintains.[286] It was not without good reason that instead of the animal whose pelt was removed, undoubtedly in a ritualistic practice, a mythological fantasy-creature was named. This avoidance of the animal's name agrees with the strong "taboo" (so called by the English scholars whom we shall be citing shortly) placed on the *goat* in the cult of Athene.

It would be less rigid and more accurate to the possible nuances of the phenomenon if we speak of a sacred quality, one which was bound up with certain associations that had entered its field spontaneously in ancient times or were derived from the existing culture; these, moreover, could attain different degrees of intensity and meaning. There were, for instance, the degrees of the ambivalent relationship of persons to the "tabooed" object, or to the *sacrum* generally, whose two meanings, the positive and the negative, are familiar. In this relationship the positive side was hidden behind the negative. Thus Varro distinguishes between two levels of the *odium* which was aroused by the *caprinum genus* (the "race of goats"). The goat was sacrificed to Dionysos or to *Liber pater*. Other Deities did not even want to see it. To Pallas Athene nothing of it at all was offered, since even the spittle of the goat is poison to the olive tree. Therefore it is established that no goats were allowed to set foot on the Acropolis, with the exception of one particular and necessary sacrifice: *hoc nomine etiam Athenis in arcem non inigi, praeterquam semel ad necessarium sacrificium, ne arbor olea, quae primum ibi nata, a capra tangi possit.*[287]

On this Farnell [288] based his hypothesis of the ritual origin of Athene's aegis – how else could she have worn the pelt of this despised animal? – and also of the aegis of Zeus, who in Homer is the principal wearer of it. In certain Grecian cults, such as those of Dionysos and of Artemis of Brauron, the goat was a "theanthropic" animal that could equally well be identified with the God as with the sacrificer. Zeus, too, was once called *aigophagos* ("goat devourer"), and he most certainly also received goat offerings. According to Farnell, the same sacrifice for Pallas Athene must have been pre-Homeric, since in later times every connection between the Goddess and the goat disappeared. In this hypothesis, the ambivalent connection between Athene and the goat does not receive adequate attention. The aegis, he maintained, retained its magical power from the time when it was still removed from the sacrificial animal. This agrees with the conception of Frazer,[289] who on the basis of Varro's testimony believed he could assert that the goat, if it was sacrificed only once a year on the Acropolis, was sacrificed in the character of Pallas Athene herself. Later, however, he retracted this thesis, since Varro speaks only of a *necessarium sacrificium* and does not name the Deity who received it. On the Acropolis of Athens this could also have been Artemis Brauronia.[290]

This possibility could not be rejected out of hand, although we know that the animal sacrifice which Miltiades praised consisted of five hundred goats of Artemis Agrotera[291] and that these animals did not come onto the Acropolis. The goat sacrifice to Brauronia most likely took place on the spot where the Athenian maidens performed their service to the Goddess: in Brauron. Supporting this is the fact that the same sacrifice is described by a cultic legend in Munichia as a substitutionary offering for a maiden.[292] On the other hand, since we are holding firmly to the ritual origination of the aegis, both because of the ambivalent relationship of the Goddess to the *caprinum genus* and because of the stories of flaying and of the removed pelt, we do not need to grasp at such a far-reaching hypothesis as the identification of Athene with the goat. The feminine *capra* in Varro may be accidental, and even if not it gives absolutely no support for such an assertion. If Zeus (and Hera also, in Sparta) is called *aigophagos*, the devouring of goats by these Deities can be explained in a completely different way. It is sufficient here as well, simply to refer to that *odium* behind which may also be concealed a positive relationship to this eagerly slaughtered and joyfully consumed creature. Through ritual, the animal is made *serviceable* to the God or Goddess. Could this not have been the case with the goat in the cult of Athene?

As the nearest analogy to the non-martial usage of the aegis, when the priestess of Athene donned it to visit the newly married couple after the wedding night,[293] Farnell cites a Roman example: the employment of the *amiculum Iunonis* (the goatskin of Juno) in the Lupercalia festival. From the pelt were cut the thongs with which the *Luperci* served the Goddess and the women. Whether this had the same meaning as had the visit of the aegis-bearing priestess for the newly-married couples, where the prior wedding event could already have been sealed and blessed, is more than questionable. Recently it has even been questioned whether Juno had anything to do with the Lupercalia.[294] As the main argument against this clear tradition, it has been pointed out that in the Lupercalia both the sacrificial animals – goat and dog – and the celebrants themselves, were masculine. To this we add that the *flamen Dialis* was himself part of this festival, and he was otherwise not allowed even to mention the names of goat and dog[295] – which is evidence for great ambivalence in the character of this celebration. My own reflections on the wolf and goat in the Lupercalia festival, which do not rest essentially on the association of the festival with Faunus and Juno, expressed the masculine character of both the institution of the *Luperci* and their rites, although for me the essentially important thing was the evidence of interchangeability between two equal forms of expression for the masculine, the goat and the wolf.[296] But if this accentuated masculinity could be an argument against the relationship of the festival to a Goddess of women like Juno, then no relationship at all could be admitted between the masculine and the feminine, let alone an ambivalent one. The Italic parallels to the relationship of Athene with the goat are much easier to find in the cults of Juno of Falerii and Juno Sospita in Lanuvium. In Falerii there is evidence for the enmity of the Goddess against the goat and against the goat hunt held in her honor.[297] And Juno Sospita appears with goatskin on her head and shoulders, with outstretched lance and shield, in battle-position,[298] and in closest association with the serpent[299] and raven,[300] as though she were the Pallas Athene of Lanuvium.

The image of the Greek Goddess is distinguished from the Italic – which was certainly influenced by the Greek – not least of all by a richer and more subtle synthesis that reaches beyond the inner tension of the material. To this image belongs the combination of goatskin and Gorgoneion. A secret rite, to which the aegis owes its origin and at which Varro may have been hinting with his *necessarium sacrificium*, was never completely suppressed through this combination, and it was probably repeated annually in some form, whatever the meaning of the celebration may have been. This is the direction in which an examination of the archeological material leads us. The theme of the Gorgoneion is not nearly exhausted by this material, but even so it is now possible to present several points of view for a more general treatment.

The Gorgoneion is itself already the result of a synthesis. At the time when representations of the Gorgon first appear in Greek art (not earlier than the seventh century B.C.[301]), the *Gorgeiē kephalē*, the construction of the "Gorgon head," to which Homer attests, was already present. This is the presupposition of all representations: it holds together the different variations and bears the features that were in part borrowed from Oriental art, not that these could be traced back without remainder to an extra-Greek model.[302] As we said, it is a construction, the result of a synthesis that in addition to the serpent motif united at least three other ethnologically widely-dispersed motifs: first, the motif of the head which has been taken as booty;[303] then, the motif of the winged disk,[304] or of a winged Deity with a disk-face;[305] third, the motif of the mask. The terrorizing motif was always bound up with the mask, and this was further heightened by its combination with the motif of the severed head, which grimaces with tongue out-stretched. The disk-face has this dark and horrifying expression. The same disk can, however, of itself be bright. Actually the *bright* Medusa is even *archaic*.[306] So much does the femininity of the Gorgon or the Gorgons, these Goddesses with disk-faces, dominate the employment of the flat-pressed head as mask that I believed (certainly not without justification)

I could recognize in the Gorgon head the feminine prototype in the history of the Greek mask (beside the masculine prototype, the Dionysos mask),[307] even if a closer approximation of this type to a masculine type also seems necessary to me.

The masculine characterization of the body on which the Gorgon's head rests[308] signifies nothing in relation to the face. This is not only because men too could wear this image as a mask, but also because the head demands a special judgment of its own, as a construction which Greek mythology displays as clearly feminine but which in itself could be apprehended also as masculine or neutral. A. Furtwängler, the best judge of the materials which were earlier available, spotted the masculine character of the Gorgon masks in what he called the "beard" of the Gorgon,[309] which is also seen wherever the face is placed on the body of a Goddess.[310] This "beard" is characteristic for a number of the very oldest Gorgon representations.[311] Its stylization varies from a beard to a row of fringes hanging down under the face. An example of the latter is the old and especially remarkable example, the "Dame aux cygnes" on the Kamiros plate. Furthermore, attention is called to a pointy-bearded bird as the Gorgon's bird on a Corinthian vase, which corresponds to a bearded male bird on a proto-Corinthian vase.[312] Such examples cause one to wonder if traces of a rite with a bearded male animal and the employment of its hide for similar purposes, as the Gorgon's head was used later, did not from the beginning belong to the elements of this compound-faced creature.

This possibility is raised to a certain level of probability by the fact that a prototypical Gorgoneion – most likely the oldest example of all, dating to the first half of the seventh century[313] – wore *horns*: *"petites cornes placées sur le front*."[314] The horns are not so simply directed upward, as were those in the clearest example of this type known to Furtwängler, in the Akroterion mask of Sparta.[315] These are twisted in a generally upwards direction and are therefore a goat's or ram's horns. Supposing they were rams' horns – a pseudo-scientific variant on the history of the animal called "Aegis" held that the Gorgon was a wild sheep with poisonous breath[316] – this still would not alter the observation that the Gorgoneion was not merely an apotropaic device but rather a form of earlier ritualistic dress in animal skin and animal mask.[317] The nearest relative to this among the masculine types of mask is the Silenos mask.[318] This mask is embellished with weapons as apotropaic instruments just as is the Gorgoneion,[319] and it appeared at the festival of Apaturia in Athens, most likely at the point of getting dressed in the pelt of the sacrificed goat.[320] What is more, Athene, in her character as Phratria, received the sacrifice at this festival, along with Zeus Phratrios.[321]

The image of the *he-goat* completed the series of animal forms in which the paternal-masculine partner of the virginal-maternal Goddess could appear. The other two images were the serpent and the bull. Outside of the Acropolis of Athens, the stallion appeared as a variant, like the Silenoi beside the satyr. In the relatively late prehistoric period, the Goddess herself may have sometimes taken the form of a mare – or of the Gorgon.

So various were the masks of the Divine, playing in man and playing around him, for him.

Murray Stein

TRANSLATOR'S AFTERTHOUGHTS

This translation of Karl Kerényi's essay on Pallas Athene adds to the series in English of his studies of Greek Gods and Goddesses. This series now includes his works on Asklepios (*Archetypal Image of the Physician's Existence*, 1959); Dionysos (*Archetypal Image of Indestructible Life*, 1976); Demeter and Persephone (*Eleusis: Archetypal Image of Mother and Daughter*, 1967); Hermes (*Guide of Souls*, 1976); Prometheus (*Archetypal Image of Human Existence*, 1963); Zeus and Hera (and Poseidon) (*Archetypal Image of Father, Husband and Wife*, 1975). Still untranslated are works on Apollo, Orpheus, and also on Telesphoros, not to mention other studies on various figures and themes in Greek myth and religion. (All told, Kerényi published some forty-five works between the 1930's and the early 1970's, of which about ten have now been translated into English.) One hopes that all of his works will someday be available to English-reading audiences. The complete product is a most impressive *opus* of scholarship and interpretation.

The author defines this essay as a study in the history of religions. This is its genre. But since the focus of attention is fixed not directly on the elucidation of the history of religious thought and practice in the cults of Pallas Athene, but rather on the object of those cults' veneration, namely the Goddess herself, the essay is more precisely defined as a study in the history of the Gods (p. 4). It is, therefore, *also* an analysis of an archetypal image, a fact which does not exclude its contribution to historical understanding. This approach is itself an important methodological contribution to the field known as history of religions, and it requires more of the scholar than is usually expected or demanded (p. 2).

Kerényi compares his work to that of an archeologist. As a student of past human experience of an archetypal image, he digs and sifts through ancient monuments and remains of a once clearly defined religious cult. To understand this image and the experience of it, he seeks to reconstruct it and the cultic practices associated with it. Kerényi is quite conscious of the fact that this act of reconstruction from the "fragments" as these exist for us today is itself a myth-making act. The image that emerges from this reconstruction is based on the objective data made available by rigorous scholarship, but the nuances and emphases that bring it to life and give it coherency are based in the imagination and judgment of the reconstructor. The final product, therefore, is at least partially *Kerényi's* myth of Pallas Athene. Archeologists, too, sift, weigh, judge, and then imagine, in creating their reconstructions of the past. This is true of any profession that is in the business of making interpretations, whether it be the profession of historian, archeologist, or psychologist. To interpret is to create.

Kerényi cautions the reader not to expect a pleasurably smooth text, an enjoyable retelling of an ancient story. This is not an historical novel, and it does not read like one. It is a work of painstaking scholarship, as even a brief glance at the footnotes will indicate. Like Kerényi's other works, this essay cannot be read speedily. His style is complex and indirect, his path weaves in and out rather than running straight ahead in a narrative or expository manner, and themes often seem to get lost in a welter of detail. His works need more than one reading, and the act of understanding them is itself a creative work. He shows more the reservation and appreciation for ambiguity of the scholar than the practical straightforwardness and certainty of the storyteller. Nor does he share with his great mentor, Walter Otto, the tendency toward romanticism and poetic flight: in musical terms, Kerényi prefers atonality and dissonance where Otto preferred romantic harmony and the grand Beethoven sweep.

This work on Athene should not, however, be construed as pure scholarship. It is highly interpretive, as the author assembles a coherent image from the mass of data which thousands of hours of scholarly effort have unearthed. What this mythopoeic work offers to the patient and attentive reader is an understanding of a coherent, though by no means simplified or poeticized, archetypal image. If Greek myths help us to work out our confusions about the soul, Kerényi helps us to understand these sortings-out.

TRANSLATOR'S AFTERTHOUGHTS

The key to Kerényi's understanding and interpretation of Pallas Athene lies in his explanation of the paradox that she is at once both divine *Virgin* and divine *Mother*. Other scholarly interpreters of Greek religion and mythology could not have missed this peculiar self-contradiction within the image, but they have chosen to pass over it in favor of highlighting other characteristics of the Goddess. For Otto, whom Kerényi quotes with appreciation in this essay, the distillate of all the facts about Pallas Athene is clear-eyed sagacity, intelligence directed toward practical, concrete goals, the "Metis" aspect of her being. Kerényi, however, fixes on the paradoxical, conflicted qualities in Athene's nature and on the implications of these inner contradictions for our understanding of this image. On the one hand, Athene is divine Protectress and Mother; on the other hand, she is divine Virgin and Martial Maid (cf. Carol Rupprecht, "The Martial Maid," *Spring 1974*). How can these contrary opposites be fused in one figure? And what is the meaning of this fusion? These are the questions he addresses.

The title of Kerényi's essay on Athene naturally leads us to associate this mythologem with a Christian counterpart, the Virgin Mary. The parallels are striking, but the differences are equally important. Both figures are virginal mothers; both are primarily committed to the spirit of the Father; both soften and mediate the spirit of the archaic Father; both are concerned with mercy and justice. Athene, however, is not a *theotokos* ("God-bearer") in the sense that Mary is, nor does she show the same attitude of unambivalent receptivity to the Father. The tonal quality surrounding Athene is more defensive, more militant, and more supportive of heroic striving. One could speculate that the countries of northern Europe (and of Protestantism) inherited more of the spirit of Pallas Athene, while the countries of southern Europe (and of Catholicism) received and cultivated more the spirit of the Christian Virgin-Mother. The receptive maternal elements in Pallas Athene, while present, are more subdued and hidden in the background, behind her defensive armaments, than is the case with the Virgin Mary. With the Virgin Mary the maternal flame, the glowing womb, is prominent; with Pallas Athene it is concealed. This describes a difference in soul-quality between Protestantism and Catholicism.

For Kerényi, the center of gravity in the image of Athene lies neither in her "Metis aspect" nor in her motherhood, but in her bondedness to the

Father. This perspective opens the mythologem to further and deeper analysis than did the earlier emphasis of his teacher, Walter Otto, upon which René Malamud based his study, "The Amazon Problem" (*Spring 1971*).

Kerényi argues that the virginal-maternal paradox in the image of Pallas Athene is intelligible if one gives sufficient weight to her relationship with the Father. The father-daughter mythologem lies at the base of the Athene religion, and the ramifications emanating from this base determine the contradictions in her nature. Because of this bond she will give herself to no husband, yet because of this bond she must become a mother in order to supply the paternal order with future generations. Her role as mother, therefore, represents a contribution to the interests of the Father and his order. Both requirements demand sacrifice: in her cult virgins are both honored and sacrificed, either literally for the protection and well-being of the fatherland, or symbolically as they are initiated into marriage and motherhood for the purpose of generating and maintaining the future. Unlike Otto, Kerényi does not evade this dark side of the image. And yet always the brightness of virginity is restored, like the moon passing through darkness into rebirth: the marriage is consummated, the child is born, and virginity is restored as the mother presents the child to the line of generations begotten by and for the father and returns to his side.

One accent in the mythologem to which Kerényi pays special attention is the theme of defense. Pallas Athene is a Protectress, a Defender of persons and cities. What she defends, according to Kerényi, are the prerogatives, the interests, the spirit of the Father, "father-right" as he terms it. And what she defends against is any force that would "invade" or challenge these strongholds of the paternal spirit. This would lead us to the deceptively misleading surmise that the forces she defends against must originate with the angry Mothers who had been deposed and sealed off from the areas of legitimate consciousness by the victorious spirit of patriarchal supremacy. But as Kerényi takes great pains to demonstrate, her relationship to the Father is extremely ambiguous. Was she violated by him? Is the Gorgoneion the skin of the revengefully murdered father? Is her defensiveness really focused against the archaic father and his overwhelming phallic spirit? Before trying to meditate on these questions, we need to grasp the psychological quality of Athenean defense.

We are following Jung now: taking back and in the projection represented by the mythologem of Pallas Athene and looking for her ways and her force in psychological life as a power that motivates fantasy, feelings, and behavior. In making this move, though, we do not forget that we are dealing with a Goddess, a *daimon* (*CW9*, ii, § 51): her defensive, as well as her other aspects, reach us with the quality of absolute power and compelling force. When this is the case, we become *worshippers* of a Goddess, of the *daimon* which can be identified as Pallas Athene. Paying attention to her, we perform a *religio*.

The attitude symbolized by Athene is clearly a partial reflection of the spirit of the Father (at least in his Zeus-aspect). In the reflection, however, certain aspects of the Father are screened out and the quality of this spirit is changed. To what kind of spirit will we gain access if we approach Spirit through Athene? Here Otto's insights into Athene's nature can help us. Kerényi agrees with Otto on the "spiritual" (i.e., mental) nature of the facts surrounding Athene, but this spirit needs to be distinguished from, say, the spirit of an Apollo or from the spirit of Zeus himself. Otto demonstrates, and Kerényi would have to agree, that the spirit of Athene is of a kind that is aimed at handling practical affairs in an heroic, also in an intelligent and clever, way. Athene's version of spirit is embodied in her favorite heroes: men of practical affairs, winners on the battlefield and in the forum, enterprising men of business and leaders in military enterprises. Athene supports the spirit of strategic planning for the achievement of heroic (not necessarily ideal) goals. She fosters reflection – not the kind of reflection that leads to insight for its own sake, but reflection that aims at more certain victory. Athene's spirit is the spirit of achievement, competence, action in the world: she gets us out there to win, and gives us the heart to do so, and the wit. It is hard to keep from seeing Athene in the American statue of liberty and in the American spirit of enterprise, in American expansionism, military heroics and Pentagon planning (note Kerényi's observations on her subtle connection with Ares), and in American football (especially in the position of the quarterback, the strategist).

Athene keeps us in the "real world"; she gives us the wherewithall to confront its problems, the joy of conquering ourselves, others, problems, and the sagacity and confidence to slay its dragons. She keeps us grounded in "real projects," out of vain and idle speculations. As a religious attitude,

Athene is muscular and action-oriented: building, winning, marching. We can see her moving in the religion of the "healthy-minded," to use the phrase of William James, and not in the religion of "sick souls" who pass through the terrors of guilt and breakdown into visions of transcendence. As philosopher she is pragmatic, giving "wise counsel" to those who reflect on strategies for action.

For good and ill, the spirit of Athene enters therapy, or perhaps works to convert analysis into therapy, as analyst or analysand (or both) becomes compulsively interested in "improvement," ego-building, action, heroic striving, patient effort for concrete results. Everything else becomes regression or is seen as defense against the "real issues." There is a demand to translate thought into action, to leave off wallowing in conflicts for decision, to convert insights into improved ego-defenses. Behind this also lies threat: the frightful aegis-Gorgoneion combination, persecuting with diagnostic labels those who drop out or are not up to the heroic battle. The "positive transference" may be exemplified by the analysand who connects to the Athenean attitude that informs the analyst. Or, the presence of Athene in therapy may reinforce, rather than challenge, an Athene mother-complex, which clinically looks very different from what one usually understands by "mother-complex." But Athene is a kind of mother, and by realizing that she too can appear as mother-complex we can sort out different varieties of that complex, varieties that begin to look more like opposites than relatives.

The mythologem of Pallas Athene offers us an opportunity, then, to gain insight into the defensive nature of heroic striving and into the complexities of defense.

On the one hand, Athene supplies strategic reflection to be used against the threat of the horrible Mother: the reflecting shield of Perseus, which he uses to slay Medusa, is a gift of Athene; she also aids crucially in the rescue of Orestes from the persecution of the implacable Furies, who symbolize the 'awe-ful' defense of mother-right; she whispers counsel to Achilles as he is about to be overcome by blind rage. So, she defends against madness, overwhelming affect, psychotic loss of ground to the powers "below," against the "intolerable image" in the spider web at the bottom of the psyche. Here the defense is *distantiation*, through reflection and "cutting off." It is a defense of reflective distance and repression through intellectualization.

On the other hand, Athene defends against the dark aggressiveness of the Father. As Kerényi makes clear, Athene's relationship to the figure of the father is highly ambivalent and colored by the theme of rapacious incest. The archaic father appears in this mythologem as forceful seducer, as rapist and murderer. Here Athene defends against loss of feminine choice and integrity, against the power of the paternal phallus to bind the daughter in eternal infantilism and fear of his harsh and absolute domination, against the attacking and undermining force of the archaic masculine. In this, her defense is "identification with the aggressor": Athene puts on the father's aegis, wears the Gorgoneion, practically becomes the Father. Thus the force of the masculine is absorbed and converted into a kind of masculine forcefulness of the father's daughter. To defend herself from him, she becomes like him; in his pride, then, he may protect rather than attack her. Identification with the aggressor may look like a defensive failure. Has not the father won, after all? In a sense he has. Athene becomes a defender of the patriarchal order and is bound to imitation of the father's spirit, but in this his archaic elements are deflected from his daughter. These aggressive elements can now be directed elsewhere. The father, meanwhile, is seduced into trusting and protecting this daughter who is so much like himself. Her defense, aimed toward fending off the archaic elements of the father and to do this by advancing and supporting his more "spiritual" side, also includes *denial*: the mysterious child born to Athene is secretely whisked off in the dead of night, so as to preserve (or restore) her pristine virginity and to secure her position as the father's "spiritual" alter-ego.

There *is* a dark night among the cultic celebrations of Athene, and there *is* a passage through affliction. All is not bright-eyed heroic striving. We come upon the poignancy and depth in the image when we look carefully into what is being defended. We must face the conundrum that the father's daughter is protecting neither her virginity *per se* nor (which amounts to the same thing) her privileged relationship with the father. Her closeness to him and her identification with him are themselves defenses against his archaic threats to her womanhood. But because she has used the defense of identification-with-the-aggressor, she has no means left open for full expression of her womanhood. This is the trap of the soul which has chosen the defense of heroic striving against the threat of the persecution of the archaic father. What is being protected by Pallas is expressed in the image of the small flame in the fire-pan, which according to Kerényi explains the name Athene. Pallas protects Athene. What she protects, therefore, is a core of womanhood as it finds itself besieged by the archaic spirit of the father. And since all men represent father to her, none can be allowed into her womb. Her womb, while not barren literally, remains inviolate psychologically: hence, she is both mother (literally) and virgin (psychologically). Her literal mothering is performed for the fatherland, while her psychological (soul-full) mothering is reserved for the children never born to this world. This is one meaning of Athene's connection to Persephone and to the fertility of the realm of unborn souls. This hiatus between the literal and the psychological, between deed and meaning, generates the pathos of achieving "real" goals that don't count for the soul, sublimated and substitutionary goals, even while the womb is literally productive, the career literally successful, and heroic striving literally in high gear. Heroic striving and its results do not satisfy because they are fundamentally defensive in nature.

Heroic striving and conquering can be insighted from many different mythologems: the Promethian variety as rebellion and self-assertion; the Herculean variety as escape from and defense against the persecuting mother; the variety of Perseus who conquers for the sake of the mother, etc. The military stridency of the Athenean version is its distinguishing feature, and its defense against the archaic father is primary. It would be a mistake to see Athene only in heroic striving however, or only as the pattern of a common neurotic defense, although everything else that is said about her must be considered with this in mind. As an agent transformative of the archaic elements of the masculine spirit, her defensive posture is necessary for the safe flourishing of civilized life in the *polis*.

A function of Athene, which Kerényi does not stress but which derives from her being a transformative mediator of the masculine spirit and protectress against the ravaging impulse of its archaic elements, is that of teacher: she teaches mankind the arts of weaving, pottery, metallurgy, ship-building, and yoking oxen. All of these are practical arts, crafts; Athene is a teacher, therefore, not in the sense of guru or wise woman, but of helpful guide in the arts and crafts which civilize human life and which harness and contain "the lawless powers belonging to the world of darkness" (Jung, *CW9*, ii, § 60). With Athene, and for her, we weave a *peplos*, whether we are writing, cultivating, or "getting it together" in the turbulence of our lives. She keeps us patiently, craftily at it until the garment is pieced together, thread on thread, warp to woof, until it's "right."

Psychologically, then, Athene protects our civilized and civilizing selves from the consuming fires of the spirit (could mystics build a city?) and from the threats of our various primordial passions (look at what Dionysos did to Thebes). Like her craftsmen, the metallurgists, she "tempers." Athens, one of the glories of the civilized self, is, after all, her namesake.

One of the major strengths of Kerényi's treatment of Athene is that he stays with the ambiguity of the Goddess's reality, just as archetypal psychology must stay with the tensions and ambiguities of psychological life. No God or Goddess is without pathology, as no pathology is without its God (cf. James Hillman, "On the Necessity of Abnormal Psychology," *Eranos-43*, 1974). Archetypal psychology moves both ways, locating psyche in myth and myth in psyche.

NOTES AND REFERENCES

1 Kerényi, K., "Die Entstehung der Olympischen Götterfamilie," in the journal *Paideuma*, VI, 1950, pp. 127ff (note that on p. 128, line 17, there is a disturbing typographical error, where "not" should be omitted). Kerényi, "Zeus und Hera," in the journal *Saeculum*, I, 1950, pp. 228ff.

2 *Iliad*, II, 371; IV, 288; VII, 132; VI, 97; *Odyssey*, VII, 311; XVIII, 235; XXIV, 376. The trinity Zeus-Hera-Athene is infrequent: Pausanias, X, 5, 2.

3 *Iliad*, XIII, 825. Translation by Richard Lattimore, Chicago and London, 1951.

4 Nilsson, M. F., *Geschichte der griechischen Religion*, I, München, 1941-50, p.400.

5 Kerényi, C., *Zeus and Hera*, translated by Christopher Holme, Princeton, 1975, pp. 114ff.

6 Duemmler, F., *Athena: Kleine Schriften*, II, Leipzig, 1901, p. 75 and in Pauly, A., and Wissowa, G. (eds.), *Real-Encyclopädie der classischen Altertumswissenschaft*, Stuttgart, 1898ff (hereafter referred to as Pauly-Wissowa).

7 Kerényi, *Zeus and Hera*, p. 116.

8 Nilsson, pp. 323ff.

9 Cf. below, pp. 17f and pp. 50f.

10 Moritz, K. Ph., *Götterlehre oder mythologische Dichtung der Alten*, in many editions since 1791, the latest 1948, Lahr, Schwarzwald.

11 Rückert, E., *Der Dienst der Athena*, Hildburghausen, 1829, pp. 192ff.

12 Hesiod, *Theogony*, 896.

13 Duemmler, pp. 80ff.

14 Gill, W. W., *Myths and Songs from the South Pacific*, 1876, p. 10; referred to by Otto, W., *The Homeric Gods*, translated by Moses Hadas, N.Y., 1944, p. 36.

15 Kerényi, *Zeus and Hera*, p. 96.

16 Hesiod, *Theogony*, 887.

17 Cf. the two versions in Kerényi, *The Gods of the Greeks*, translated by Norman Cameron, London, 1961, pp. 118ff. Both were rejected by Wilamowitz-Moellendorf, Ulrich von, in *Athena*, Sitz. -Ber., Berlin, 1921, p. 957.

18 Cf. the text in Güterbock, H., *Kumarbi*, Zürich and New York, 1946, and the excerpt in the *American Journal of Archeology*, LII, 1948, p. 124.

19 Kerényi, C., "Miti sul concepimento di Dioniso," in the journal *Maia*, IV, 1951, pp. 1ff; Kerényi, C., *Dionysos*, translated by Ralph Manheim, Princeton, 1976, pp. 35f.

20 Kern, O. (ed.), *Orphica Fragmenta* (1922), 85.

21 Hesiod, *Theogony*, 358.

22 Toepffer, J., *Attische Genealogie*, Berlin, 1889, p. 165.

23 "Archaic Cult in Thespiai," Pausanias, IX, 27, 1; also, cf. Nilsson, p. 187.

24 Nilsson, p. 458.

25 *Ibid.*, p. 461.

26 Euripides, *The Heracleidae*, 770-72, where *gas* is (with Murray) to be removed and not (with Dieterich) converted into *Ga*, Mother Earth; cf. Wilamowitz, *Hermes*, XVII, pp. 356ff.

27 Kerényi, *Zeus and Hera*, p. 237.

28 Pausanias, V, 3, 2.

29 Cf. below, note 293, for a comment on Nilsson's critique.

30 Deubner, L., *Attische Feste*, Berlin, 1932, p. 16.

31 Plutarch, *Numa*, 9.

32 Brückner, A., *Athenische Mitteilungen*, XXXII, 1907, pp. 114ff.

33 Weinreich, O., *Der Trug des Nektanebos*, Leipzig, 1911, pp. 34ff.

34 Cf. note 44, for a comment opposing the assumption of primordial promiscuity and opposing Bachofen's conception of Athene. On the schema "Hetairism-Matriarchy-Patriarchy," cf. Kerényi, "Zu J. J. Bachofens Porträt," *Neue Schweizer Rundschau*, N. F. 19, 1952, pp. 676ff.

35 Cf. Kerényi, C., "Man and Mask," in *Spiritual Disciplines* (Papers from the Eranos Yearbooks, 4, translated by Ralph Manheim), New York, 1960, pp. 162ff.

36 Deubner, pp. 232ff.

37 Plato, *Euthyphro*, 302d.

38 Harpocration, s.v. *lampas*.

39 Pausanias, II, 33, 1.

40 Deubner, p. 16.

41 Antigonus, *Scriptores Rerum Mirabilium Graeci* (ed. Westermann, 1839), 12; Michaelis, A. T. F., and Jahn, O., *Arx Athenarum a Pausania Descripta,* Bonn, 1901, pp. 2ff.

42 Plutarch, *Comparatio Aristophanis et Menandri*, 773: *schedon eurōn tas duo phuseis tou te patros kai tēs mētros.*

43 Jacoby, F. (ed.), *Fragmente der griechischen Historiker*, II, 319, fragment 49.

44 Varro *ap*. St. Augustine, *The City of God*, XVIII, 9. Cf. Bachofen, J. J., *Das Mutterrecht*, I, Basel, 1948, p. 171. The comment of the editor Meuli (1109, 4) is correct: Bachofen never considers the idea that an autochthonous agricultural population could have been matriarchal and the invading Indo-Germanic tribes patriarchal. The picture which presents itself to us is even more complicated and nuanced. The assumption of an original promiscuity is not supported by any ethnological analogies: cf. Thurnwald, R., "Promiscuität" in M. Ebert's *Reallexikon der Vorgeschichte*, p. 320, and cf. also the entry "Ehe."

45 Nilsson, p. 325.

46 Cook, A. B., *Zeus*, II, Cambridge, 1914-40, pp. 1091ff.

47 Hippocrates, *De Insomnia*, IV; Cook, p. 1054.

48 Nilsson, p. 325.

49 Kerényi, *The Gods of the Greeks*, translated by Norman Cameron, London and New York, 1974[3], p. 113 and pp. 250ff.; also, Kerényi, "Miti sul concepimento di Dioniso," pp. 7ff.

50 Eusebius, *Praeparatio Evangelica*, X, 9, 22.

51 Pausanias, VIII, 2, 3.

52 Prott, J. de, and Ziehen, L., *Leges graecorum sacrae e titulis collectae*. Leipzig, 1896-1902, pp. 46ff.N.26B13. Also, Kerényi, *Zeus and Hera*, p. 105.

53 Fehrle, E., *Die kultische Keuschheit im Altertum*, Giessen, 1910, p. 201. Nilsson (p. 416) stresses the remarkable fact that the epithet Meter was, except for Demeter, applied to no Goddess other than Ge. What Parthenos signifies as a special nominal description of a Goddess is in Athens always understood as Athene.

54 Cf. Frickenhaus, A., *Athenische Mitteilungen*, XXXIII, 1908, pp. 17ff., and Buschor, E., *ibid.*, XLVII, 1922, p. 96.

55 Solinus, IX, 8; Kerényi, *The Gods of the Greeks*, p. 147.

56 Fehrle, pp. 162ff.

57 Preller, L., *Griechische Mythologie*, I. edited by C. Robert, Berlin, 1887-1926, p. 328, 5n.

58 Nilsson, p. 410.

59 Harding, M. E., *Woman's Mysteries: Ancient and Modern*, London-New York-Toronto, 1938, p. 268.

60 *Homeric Hymn to Aphrodite*, 7-8.

61 Cf. Kerényi, "Mythologisches Mädchenbildnis," in the journal *Du*, Zürich, 1949, Nr. 5, and Kerényi, "A Mythological Image of Girlhood," *Spring 1969*, pp. 93ff.

62 *Iliad*, V, 875, 880.

63 Hesiod, *Theogony*, 924-25. Translation by Richmond Lattimore in his *Hesiod*, University of Michigan Press, 1973.

64 It is not certain how the adjective *atrutōnē* is to be translated.

65 Pindar, *Olympia*, VII, 36.

66 Walter Otto is correct in *The Homeric Gods*, translated by Moses Hadas, New York, 1954, p. 44.

67 *Iliad*, XXI, 403.

68 *Ibid.*, XVIII, 516.

69 Apollodorus, III, 14, 2.

70 Pausanias, VII, 22.

71 As Enyalios and as Ares: Pollux, VIII, 105.

72 Pausanias, III, 15, 5.

73 Apollodorus, III, 15, 8.

74 See below, p. 27.

75 Livy, XLII, 51.

76 Rodenwaldt, G., *Athenische Mitteilungen*, XXXVII, 1912, pp. 129ff.; also, Nilsson, p. 324 with Plate 24, 1.

77 Otto, *The Homeric Gods*, p. 43.

78 *Ibid.*, pp. 56, 57, 60.

79 Compare *pallax* ("boy" and "girl") with *pallakē*, *pallakis* ("concubine").

80 Eustathius, *Commentaria ad Iliadem et Odysseam* (ed. G. Stallbaum, 1825-30), pp. 84, 1419, 1742.

81 Sophocles, fragment 872, in Nauck, A. (ed.), *Tragicorum graecorum fragmenta*, Leipzig, 1889, p. 392.

82 Nilsson, p. 408; cf. also Lippold, G., "Palladion," in Pauly-Wissowa, 190ff.

83 Apollodorus, III, 12, 3; also, Kerényi, *The Gods of the Greeks*, p. 122.

84 Kerényi, *ibid.*, p. 120.

85 Megamedeides or Megamedeios; perhaps Megamedes was an epithet of the

Hesiodian Titan Krios.

86 Hesiod, *Theogony*, 384.

87 Cicero, *De Natura Deorum*, III, 59; scholia on Lycophron, 355.

88 Apollodorus, I, 6, 2; cf. below, p. 63.

89 Clement of Alexandria, *Protrepticus*, II, p. 24P; Arnobius, *Adversus Nationes*, IV, 14, 16; Eustathius, *ad Iliadem*, VI, 91.

90 Dionysius Halicarnassensis, *Antiquitates Romanae*, I, 33 and 68.

91 Cf. above, pp. 20 and 27.

92 Kerényi, *The Gods of the Greeks*, pp. 122ff.

93 Stephanus Byzantius, s. v. *Alalkomenion*.

94 Nilsson, pp. 406ff.

95 Cf. also *ibid*., p. 406.

96 Kretschmer, P., *Glotta*, XI, 1921, pp. 282ff.

97 *Corpus Glossarium*, II, 2, 25, and 47.

98 Hesychius, s. v.

99 Opposed also is Nilsson, p. 406, 5n.

100 Cf. the passages in Deubner, p. 35.

101 Deummler, pp. 52ff.; Nilsson, p. 412.

102 Pausanias, I, 14, 6.

103 This has to do not with the weaving of the Goddess's *peplos*, but with the craft of wool-working as a gift of the Goddess to mankind. Cf. the ceremony with the woolen garment under *prọtonion* in *Suda* and in Photius, *Bibliotheca*. On the prohibition against sacrificing an unshorn lamb, cf. Athenaeus, *Athenaeum*, IX, p. 375, and Müller, K. O., *Kleine lateinische und deutsche Schriften*, II, Göttingen, 1839, p. 153.

104 Cf. Kondoleon, N. M., *To Erechtheion*, Athens, 1949, p. 87.

105 Cf. the passages in Ziehen, L., "Palladion," in Pauly-Wissowa, 172.

106 Apollodorus, III, 12, 3.

107 Lippold, "Palladion," in Pauly-Wissowa, 194ff. The tale of the doubling of the Trojan Palladium belongs here also, since it has to do not with two identical, but with two differently formed, Palladiums. The Athenian copy shows a difference, and this has a bearing on the difference between the two aspects. The one image carried a frightful Gorgon on the shield, the other a beautiful one: the dark and bright aspects stand next to each other. Literature on the two Palladiums can be found in: Mylonas, K. D., *Ephemeris Archaiologikē*, III, 1890, pp. 1ff.; Svoronos, I. N., *Das athenische Nationalmuseum*, Text I, Athens, 1908, pp. 109ff.; Papaspiridi, S., *Guide du Nationale Museum Athen*, 1929, p. 33. The well-known parallels of a double Pan and the doubled Kybele suggest that behind such doublings stand two aspects of the moon. The dark moon as Gorgon's head is confirmed, in Kern, O. (ed.), *Orphica Fragmenta*, 33.

108 Perdrizet, P., *Mélange Perrot*, 1902, pp. 259ff.

109 Heliodor in Harpocration, s. v. *Nikē Athēna.*

110 Deubner, p. 35.

111 Kerényi, "Miti sul concepimento di Dioniso," pp. 10ff.

112 *The Homeric Hymn to Demeter*, 372.

113 Apollodorus, I, 5, 3; II, 5, 12; Ovid, *Metamorphoses*, V, 259ff.

114 Deubner, pp. 17 and 40, where the Skira festival is included among the Demeter and Kore festivals.

115 Cf. p. 56 below, for more on the Arretophoria in the Skira festival.

116 Strabo, IX, 411.

117 Plato, *Laws*, 796b: *ē par ēmin korē kai despoina.*

118 Cf. Farnell, L. R., *The Cults of the Greek States*, I, Oxford, 1896-1909, Plate XIVb; Gerhard, E., *Auserlasene griechische Vasenbilder*, Berlin, 1840-58, p. 242. Cf. further in Frickenhaus, *Athenische Mitteilungen*, XXXIII, 1908, p. 21, who underscores as the most important statement of the inscriptions: *phialē chrusē ēn en tēi cheiri eschei.*

119 Blinkenberg, C., *Die Lindische Tempelchronik*, Bonn, 1915, pp. 6, 10, 12.

120 Scholium on Lycophron, 1141; Farnell, I, p. 383.

121 Originally the words *ei mē nuktōr* were probably meant to be connected to *tēi de theōi ou prosērchonto.*

122 Porphyry, *De Abstinentia*, II, 56.

123 *Ibid.*, II, 54.

124 Above, p. 23f.

125 Cf. Voigt, F. S., *Beiträge zur Mythologie des Ares und der Athena*, Leipziger Studien IV, 1881, pp. 254.

126 *Etymologicum Magnum*, s. v. *koura*; Collitz, H., *Sammlung der griechischen Dialekt-inschriften*, I, Göttingen, 1899, p. 143, Nr. 373; Solmsen, *Zeitschrift für Sprachforschungen*, XXIX, 1888, pp. 128ff.; Harrison, Jane, *Themis*, London, 1912, p. 337, 1n; Magniens, V., "Le Marriage chez les Grecs: Conditions Premières," in *Melange Franz Cumont*, Bruxelles, 1936, p. 319.

127 Cf. below, p. 36.

128 Apollodorus, III, 12, 3.

129 *Inscriptiones Graecae*, II, 1006, 10; 1011, 10; Photios, in Deubner, p. 19, 2n; probably correctly understood by Farnell, I, p. 261.

130 Photios, *Bibliotheca*, s. v. *Kalluntēria*; Hesychius, s. v. *Aglauros* and *Pluntēria.*

131 Toepffer, p. 133.

132 Ovid, *Metamorphoses*, II, 819. A seated statue is created, corresponding to the oldest seated image of Polias: cf. above, p. 20.

133 Above, p. 32.

134 Pausanias, IX, 34, 2.

135 Preller, I, pp. 214ff.

136 Above, pp. 29f.

137 Cf. Hesiod, *Theogony*, 347, according to which Okeanos together with Apollo and the river Gods *andras kourizousi* ("have the young in their keeping").

138 Koria in Arcadia, Koresia in Crete. Cf. Preller, I, p. 187, 3n.

139 Apollodorus, III, 15, 5, following Euripides, *Erechtheus*, fragment 357 (ed. Nauck).

140 Cf. the passages in Frazer's edition of Apollorus (1921), III, 15, 5.

141 Apollodorus, III, 15, 8.

142 Vergil, *Aeneid*, I, 748.

143 This was the model even for Euripides, according to Wilamowitz-Moellendorff, U. von, "Aus Kydathen," *Philologische Untersuchungen*, I, Berlin, 1880, p. 126.

144 Philochorus, fragment 14, in *Epicorum Graecorum Fragmenta* (ed. G. Kinkel); Scholia on Aristides, 13; Scholia on Demosthenes, XIX, 303.

145 The passages are in Jahn-Michaelis, *Arx Athen. zu Pausanias*, I, 27, 16.

146 Pausanias, I, 27, 3.

147 Harpocration, s. v. *arrēphorein.*

148 Scholia on Euripides, *Hecuba*, 467.

149 Above, pp. 14f.

150 Above, p. 15.

151 Toepffer, p. 122.

152 Duemmler, p. 42.

153 Harpocration, s. v. *Aglauros*; Scholia on Aristophanes, *Lysistrata*, 439.

154 Pausanias, I, 18, 2.

155 Euripides, *Ion*, 274.

156 Antigonus, 12.

157 Cf. Brelich, A., *Vesta* (Albae Vigiliae, N. F. 7), Zürich, 1949, pp. 57ff.

158 *Ibid.*, pp. 48ff.

159 Pausanias, I, 26, 5.

160 *Ibid.*, I, 26, 6; Jahn-Michaelis, p. 69.

161 Pausanias, I, 27, 1; Frickenhaus, *Athenische Mitteilungen*, XXXIII, 1908, p. 172.

162 Deubner, pp. 9ff.

163 Below, p. 42.

164 Both *ersē* and *drosos* can have both meanings. Cf. Pfeiffer, R., *Callimachus*, I, Oxford, 1949 on Callimachus' poem *Hecale*.

165 *Inscriptiones Graecae*, I, 783; Hesychius, s. v. *Erros.*

166 Kerényi, *The Gods of the Greeks*, pp. 123ff.

167 Cf. Alcam, fragment 43; Sappho, fragments 98, 12.

168 Kerényi, *Zeus and Hera*, p. 121.

169 Harpocration and Sind., s. v. *tritomēnis;* to this belongs also Kallisthenes, fragment 52 (ed. Jacoby) as Scholium on Lycophron.

170 Proclus, *In Platonis Timaeum commentarii*, 17b p. 26, 18 Di; Scholia on Plato, *Republic*, 327a.

171 Scholia on the *Iliad*, VIII, 39.

172 Suidas, s. v. *tritogenēs.*

173 Euripides, *Heracleidae*, 778.

174 Cf. Nilsson, M. P., *Die Entstehung und religiöse Bedeutung des griechischen Kalenders*, Lund, 1918, p. 26.

175 The duration of the great festivals was usually four days, of the lesser festivals one or two days. Cf. Deubner, pp. 23ff.

176 Euripides, *Heracleidae*, 777-783.

177 The name of the Charity *Kleta* is to be explained in the same way. Cf. Kerényi, *Niobe: Neue Studien über Religion und Humanität*, Zürich, 1949, pp. 31ff.

178 Kerényi, *Prometheus: Archetypal Image of Human Existence*, translated by Ralph Manheim, New York, 1963, p. 56.

179 Euripides, *Ion*, 274 and 495-96.

180 Above, p. 34.

181 Athenagoras, *Legatio pro Christianis*, I, 120, 8.

182 Above, p. 34.

183 Deubner, p. 21.

184 *Ibid*., pp. 17ff.

185 Kerényi, *Niobe*, pp. 31ff.

186 Above, pp. 33ff.

187 Sophocles, fragment 585 (ed. Nauck).

188 *Etymologicum Magnum* and Suidas, s. v. *drakaulos*.

189 Euripides, *Ion*, 496.

190 Pausanias, I, 25; Apollodorus, III, 14, 2.

191 Hyginus, *Fabulae*, 253. According to the text ("*natus est Aglaurus*"), which no modern editor has corrected, the child had to be a son. Toepffer ("Aglauros" in Pauly-Wissowa) is probably correct in assuming a mistake on the part of the Copiest. Carl Robert agrees in *Die griechische Heldensage*, I, Berlin, 1920, p. 167.

192 Apollodorus, I, 8, 5.

193 Above, p. 32.

194 Above, p. 27.

195 Euripides, *Electra*, 1258ff.; Hellanicus, fragment 38; Pausanias, I, 28, 5; *Marmor Parium*, 3.

196 Kerényi, "Miti sul concepimento," pp. 10ff.

197 Scholia on Vergil, *Georgics*, I, 12.

198 Scholia on Lychophron, 766. Cf. Robert, C., *Oidipus*, Berlin, 1915, pp. 19ff., on the indigenousness of this myth in Attica: according to him this myth was certainly not originally Thessalian and perhaps only in literature transferred to

the Thessalian Poseidon Petraios. On Hephaistos, cf. below, pp. 50ff.

199 Pausanias, I, 30, 4; Scholia on Sophocles, *Oedipus Coloneus*, 711.

200 Pausanias, V, 15, 6. In V, 15, 5 Hera is shown as being worshipped as Hippia beside Poseidon Hippios, which does not mean that this (probably) neolithic Goddess had anything to do originally with the horse.

201 This is recognized by N. Yaluris in his creditable work on Athene as Mistress of horses: *Museum Helveticum*, VII, 1950, pp. 47ff. The material which he collected does not modify the chronological sequence developed here and in earlier chapters at even one single point. Unfortunately, neither Yaluris nor Schachermeyr, in his *Poseidon und die Entstehung des griechischen Götterglaubens* (Bern, 1950), took sufficiently into account the older levels of Greek religion. My own text was written before these two works appeared.

202 Scholia on Ovid, *Ibis*, 459: "*Hippomenis filia ob stuprum equi inclusa.*" Cf. Dio Chrysostomus, *Orationes*, 32, 78; Photius and Suidas, s. v. *Parippon kai dorē*; Callimachus, fragments 94, 95 (ed. Pfeiffer).

203 Aristotle, *Athēnaiōn Politeia*, fragment 7 (ed. F. G. Kenyon); Aeschylus, *Orestes*, I, 182.

204 Cf. the appendix. The standard text on the name Leimone is the wedding of Poseidon with the Gorgon Medusa in Hesiod, *Theogony*, 279 (cf. Yaluris, pp. 58, 243); the results of this were a son in the form of a horse and a mare with the skin of Medusa.

205 Pausanias, I, 26, 5.

206 Ovid, *Metamorphoses*, II, 739.

207 Pausanias, I, 26, 5.

208 *Ibid.*; Heroditus, VIII, 55; Apollodorus, II, 14.

209 Cf. the passages in Escher's "Erechtheus," in Pauly-Wissowa, 450, where the evidence is recorded for an earlier enmity between Poseidon and Erechtheus.

210 *Iliad*, II, 547-48; Sophocles, *Aias*, 202; Herodotus, VIII, 55.

211 Schwyzer, E., *Griechische Grammatik*, I, München, 1939, p. 477.

212 For examples, cf. Kerényi, *The Gods of the Greeks*, pp. 89, 115, 171, 268.

213 Cf. Maltenx, L., *Archäologisches Jahrbuch*, XXVII, 1912, pp. 232ff.

214 Toepffer, p. 117.

215 The mother is named Zeuxippe (cf. *ibid.*, pp. 113ff.).

216 Plutarch, *Coniugalia Praecepta*, 144a.

217 Deubner, pp. 165ff.

218 On the complicated ceremony, cf. *ibid.*, pp. 159ff. and Otto, W. F., *Paideuma*, IV, Wiesbaden, 1950, pp. 111ff.

219 Deubner, pp. 26ff.

220 *Iliad*, II, 550.

221 Robert, *Die griechische Heldensage*, I, p. 352; Kerényi, *The Gods of the Greeks*, pp. 108ff.

222 Technau, W., *Archäologisches Jahrbuch*, LII, 1937, pp. 76ff. and figures 1 and 2.

223 Cf. above, p. 37.

224 Cf. above, p. 33.

225 Above, p. 38.

226 Nilsson, *Griechische Feste von religiöser Bedeutung mit Ausschluss der Attischen*, Leipzig, 1906, pp. 94ff.

227 Above, p. 25. The fourth name, Kotyto, belongs to the same sphere as does the name Baubo in the Persephone mythologem.

228 Cf. above, p. 15.

229 Harpocration, s. v.

230 Kerényi, *The Gods of the Greeks*, pp. 123ff.

231 Apollodorus, III, 14, 6.

232 Pausanias, III, 17, 3.

233 Robert, *Die griechische Heldensage*, I, pp. 229ff.

234 Pindar, *Olympian Odes*, 7, 34.

235 Cf. the passages in Jahn-Michaelis on Pausanias, I, 32, 3.

236 Kerényi, *The Gods of the Greeks*, pp. 123ff.

237 Clement of Alexandria, *Protrepticus*, II, 28, paragraph 24 P.

238 Cicero, *De Natura Deorum*, III, 55 and 57, probably following Mnaseas of Patara. Cf. J. B. Mayor's third edition, Cambridge, 1885, p. 201.

239 Cf. above, p. 40.

240 Plutarch, *Quaestiones convivales*, 741a.

241 The wordplay between Leto and *lanthanō* comes up elsewhere; cf. Plutarch in Eusebius, *Praeparatio Evangelica*, III, 1, 3.

242 Kerényi, *Niobe*, pp. 151ff.; *The Gods of the Greeks*, pp. 134ff.; Jung, C. G. and Kerényi, C., *Essays on a Science of Mythology*, translated by R. F. C. Hull, Princeton, 1969, p. 49.

243 Euripides, *Ion*, 19-27.

244 Cf. the passages in Escher's "Erichthonios," in Pauly-Wissowa, 442ff. On the artistic monuments, cf. Powell, B., *Erichthonios and the Daughters of Cecrops*, Cornell Studies 17, 1906.

245 Ovid, *Metamorphoses*, II, 750.

246 Philostratus, *Imagines*, II, 17, 6.

247 Harpocration, s. v. *arrēphorein.*

248 Apollodorus, III, 14, 6; Kerényi, *The Gods of the Greeks*, pp. 125ff.

249 Pausanias, I, 27, 3.

250 *Etymologicum Magnum*, s. v. *arrēphoroi.*

251 Suidas, s. v. *bouphonia.*

252 Harpocration, s. v.

253 There are two variants of the terms: *Arrēphoria* and *Ersēphoria*, *arrēphoroi*

and *ersēphoroi,* etc. (cf. Deubner, p. 13), the second being derived from *ersē* with the meaning of "child" (cf. above, p. 39). Besides Athene, or more exactly Herse, Ge Themis and Eileithyia too possessed "*Hersephoroi,*" and these Goddesses also had to do with new-born children.

254 Sophocles, fragment 760 (ed. Nauck). *Statois liknoisi* may very likely be related to the *phalloi* which stood among the grain swingles.

255 Deubner, p. 36, 3n.

256 Cf. Broneer, O., *Hesperia*, I, 1932, pp. 31ff.; II, pp. 329ff.; IV, pp. 109ff.

257 Scholia on Lucian, *Dialogi Meretricii*, II, 1, paragraph 276: *anapherontai de kantautha appēta iera ek steatos tou sitou kataskeuasmena mimēmata drakontōn kai andreiōn schēmatōn.* Even the source of this scholium, probably the grammarian Didymos who was a scholar of St. Augustine's time, included the Arretophoria, which he depicted in this fashion, together with the Thesmophoria and the Skirophoria, and he explained the rite, as have modern scholars, as fertility magic. But this takes into account only *one* aspect, the least religious one. Only the religious aspect could have had the *arreton*-character At first it was kept secret, though amenable to reconstruction from the details of rites and mythology; it was covered over again later through rationalistic explanations.

258 Philostratus, *Vita Apollonii*, VII, 24.

259 Hyginus, *Poetica Astronomica,* II, 13: *nascitur Erichthonius anguis...alii autem anguinea tantum crura habuisse*. According to the scholium on Plato's *Timeus*, he was *drakotopous.*

260 *Scriptores Rerum Mythicarum* (ed. Bode, G. H., 1834), III, 16: *apud Delon formam habet draconinam*, where perhaps the only mistake is the restriction to Delos. For the transformation of Apollo into a serpent, cf. Antoninus Liberalis, *Metamorphoses*, 32 (in Kerényi, *The Gods of the Greeks*, p. 141), and for the references to cultic serpents in connection with Apollo, cf. Kerényi, *Niobe*, p. 177.

261 Deubner, p. 16; van der Loeff, *Mnemosyne*, XLIV, 1916, pp. 334.

262 Cf. above, p. 15.

263 Arnobius, *Adversus Nationes*, III, 31.

264 Ister of Cyrene, fragment 24 (ed. Jacoby).

265 Kerényi, "Aidos und Themis," in *Festschrift G. van der Leeuw* (*Pro regno et sanctuario*), Nijkerk, 1950, pp. 227ff.

266 *Journal of Hellenistic Studies*, XX, 1900, XLIV.

267 Fowler, W. W., *Roman Essays and Interpretations*, Oxford, 1920, pp. 146ff.

268 Frazer, J. G., *The Golden Bough*, IV, London, 1911, p. 166, 1n.

269 Jensen, Ad. E., *Das religiöse Weltbild einer frühen Kultur*, Stuttgart, 1948; also his *Die drei Ströme*, Leipzig, 1948, especially pp. 270ff.

270 This attempt was first broached in *Annuaire de l'Institut de philologie et d'Histoire Orientales et Slaves*, IX, 9 (*Mélanges Grégoire*), pp. 299ff.

271 Ridgeway, Sir William, *The Origin of Tragedy*, Cambridge, 1910, pp. 89ff. He repeats them also in *The Early Age of Greece*, II, Cambridge, 1931, p. 432.

272 Cf. Etruscan mirror in Cook, *Zeus*, III, p. 1, following Gerhard, E., *Etruskischer Spiegel*, II, Berlin, 1845, Plate 156. It is also the basic meaning of Euripides, *Cyclops*, 360. Cf. also Nilsson, p. 409. In Etruria and in Italy generally everything archaic, even that which was taken over from Greece, was maintained in greater purity, as has been particularly demonstrated by the earlier research of F. Altheim.

273 Paley, F. A., *Euripides*, II, London, 1874, on the passage; also, Grégoire, *Euripide*, III, *Collections des Universités de France*, Paris, 1923.

274 Wilamowitz-Moellendorff, U. v., *Euripides Ion*, Berlin, 1926, on this passage.

275 The substitution of *ēixen* for the traditional *ēlthen* is a conjecture. Cf. Paley on this passage, and for the reversal of lines 992-93, cf. Grégoire.

276 Cf. above, p. 14.

277 *Iliad*, V, 741; *Odyssey*, XI, 634.

278 Frickenhaus, A., *Athenische Mitteilungen*, XXXIII, 1908, p. 17.

279 Eustathius, *ad Iliadem*, VI, 91.

280 Apollodorus, I, 6, 2.

281 Cicero, *De Natura Deorum*, III, 59.

282 Scholia on Lycophron, 355.

283 Besides the two passages cited, cf. Clement of Alexandria, *Protrepticus*, 24 P; Arnobius, *Adversus Nationes*, IV, 14; Firmicus Maternus, *De errore profanarum religionum*, 16. A very learned source is to be assumed, perhaps Mnaseas: cf. Mayor, J. B. in his edition of Cicero, *De Natura Deorum*, Cambridge, 1885, p. 201; on Mnaseas, cf. Laqueur in Pauly-Wissowa.

284 Cf. Payne, H., *Necrocorinthia*, Oxford, 1931, figures 23E, 23C, 25E, 26, 27DE.

285 Diodorus, III, 70.

286 Nilsson, p. 409.

287 Varro, *De Re Rustica*, I, 2, 19-20; cf. also Athenagoras, XIII, 578A.

288 Farnell, *Cults of the Greek States*, I, p. 100.

289 Frazer, *Golden Bough*, XIII, pp. 40ff.

290 *Ibid*., p. 41, 3n.

291 Deubner, p. 209.

292 Mommsen, A., *Feste der Stadt Athen*, Leipzig, 1898, pp. 454ff.

293 The unfounded doubt about this is to be traced back to Deubner, p. 16, and to Messerschmidt, F., *Römische Mitteilungen*, XLVII, 1932, p. 129, 2n. Nilsson's scepticism, in *Collection Latomus*, II, 1949, pp. 223ff., is also not much better justified. He refers to a Byzantine text and to the fact that Suidas first speaks of a type of hunting-aegis. But the "sacred aegis" which the priestess wears is explicitly distinguished from that one. Also proverbially this is the only one that can be spoken of.

294 This question has been raised by H. J. Rose in *Latomus*, VIII, 1949, pp. 9ff. He has to admit the possibility that the main source of our tradition, Verrius Flaccus, may not have himself invented the epithet *Iuno Februata*, which associates the Goddess with the month of Februarius and with the Lupercalia in the closest possible way (as do also *Februlis* and *Februalis*); in this case, however, the suffix of the perfect participle is supposed to be understood differently, namely, in an active sense, which as a rarity would then be more acceptable as the authority of the contemporary Roman scholar. Against the association of Faunus with the Lupercalia, it is pointed out that he does not belong within the closer confines of the city but in the wilder areas on the city's outskirts. This the Romans certainly knew too, (e.g., Verrius Flaccus), and yet they accepted his presence at

the festival. In the end Rose's critical remarks reduce the wildness and aggressiveness (which are clearly described in the sources) of the wolf-man *Luperci* to a magical pulling together of the circle against Evil, just as if there existed no other reports of wolflike men's societies from ancient and modern times: cf. Gernet, L., *Dolon le Loup*, Mélange Cumont, Bruxelles, 1936, pp. 189ff., and Höfler, O., *Kultische Geheimbünde der Germanen*, I, Frankfurt a. Main, 1934. It is exceptional that I have given attention to such exaggerated scepticism.

295 Plutarch, *Quaestiones Romanae*, 111. The participation of the Flamen Dialis is attested by Ovid in *Fasti*, II, 281-82. The omission of these features in Orsinianus may be founded on the fact that the prohibition against goats was noticed (Aulus Gellius, *Noctes Atticae*, X, 15, 12) but the inclusion was not.

296 Kerényi, *Mélanges Marouzeau*, Paris, 1948, pp. 309ff.; *Niobe*, pp. 136ff.

297 Ovid, *Amores*, III, 13, 18-22, with the interpretation of Douglas, E. M., (Mrs. van Buren), *Journal of Roman Studies*, III, 1913, p. 69: "The goat was not slain at an altar by a priest, but without the city and by several persons; i.e., it was not an ordinary sacrifice in honour of the goddess, but taboo, a sacrifice of expiation." The "sin" of the goat, according to cultic legend told by Ovid, was that it betrayed the fleeing Goddess and through this act – to complete the story – delivered her over to the pursuing man, the divine spouse.

298 Cf. the vase painting from Cerveteri, *Journal of Roman Studies*, III, 1913, p. 60, and the monuments ennumerated there by Mrs, van Buren, above all the statue in the Vatican (Helbig, W., *Führer durch die öffentlichen Sammlungen klassischer Alterthümer in Rom*, I, Nr. 301, Leipzig, 1891) and the coins.

299 For evidence, cf. Rein, E., *Die Schlangenhöhle von Lanuvium*, Commentationes F. Gustafsson, Helsinki, 1911.

300 Rein, p. 30; Haug, "Juno," in Pauly-Wissowa, 1121. On the ambivalent relation of Athene to the crow (or raven), cf. Frazer's edition of Pausanias, III, London, 1898, pp. 72ff. Related to this also is the representation of Athene on a Boeotian vase (6th C.) with shield and outstretched lance, a raven on the altar in front of her, a serpent behind her. She is receiving a procession which is leading along a mighty he-goat (Nilsson, Plate 32, 1).

301 This assertion by Fürtwangler in his article "Gorgones und Gorgon," in Roscher's *Lexikon*, 1704, still holds good today: the wide-face-masks with small mouths and large ears on Cretan seals (cf. Cook, p. 845 and Chapouthier, F., *Mélanges G. Glotz*, Paris, 1932, I, pp. 184-85) are at most "precursors" of the Gorgoneion.

302 Cf. the attempts of Pettazzoni, R., *Bollettino d'arte*, I and II, 1921-22, pp. 491ff. and Hopkins, C., *American Journal of Archeology*, XXXVIII, 1934, pp. 341ff.

303 Cf. Jensen, A. L., *Das religiöse Weltbild einer früher Kultur*, Stuttgart, 1948, pp. 73ff.

304 The finest example of this is from Olympia. The report of it is to be found in the *Jahrbuch*, XLII, 1937, Plate 13 and in Kunze, E., *Neue Meisterwerke griechischen Kunst aus Olympia*, München, 1948.

305 In addition to the Gorgon from Corfu, cf. those of Sicily and southern Italy in Orsi, P., *Monuments of Antiquity*, XXV, 1919, pp. 614ff., plate 16 and figure 211.

306 Cf. the metope of Thermos in *Antike Denkmäler*, II, V, Berlin, 1891-1931, Plates 51, 1; on the meaning of this representation, cf. Pettazzoni.

307 Kerényi, "Man and Mask," pp. 159ff.; and *Miti e Misteri*, pp. 453ff.

308 Cf. the Etruscan example, in *Archäologische Zeitung*, XXXV, 1877, Plates 11, 1.

309 Furtwängler, p. 1707.

310 Cf. the painting on a plate from Kamiros, Furtwängler's oldest example, in Nilsson, Plate 30, 2.

311 Besides the example mentioned, cf. Payne, figures 23A, B, C, D; 24A, B, C, D; as a shield-drawing of Athene on an Amasis vase, cf. *Archäologische Zeitung*, XLII, 1884, Plate 15; as combined with the aegis on the Amphora of Andokides, cf. Furtwängler, A., and Reichhold, K., *Griechische Vasenmaleriei*, München, 1904-32, Plate 133.

312 Payne, figures 12, 24A; the male bird in Johansen, H. F., *Les vases Sicyoniens*, Paris-Copenhagen, 1923, Plates 38, 4 and in Karo, G., *Strena Helbigiana*, Leipzig, 1900, p. 147. Here reference is made to A. B. Cook's thesis (pp. 837ff.): he believed that the earlier Athene, who was worshipped in the form of a serpent or an owl, wore "the exuviae of the animal that once she was. As a Snake, she dons the scaly skin with its baleful head. As an Owl, the feathered skin with its round glittering eyes... Since the skin most commonly worn was the rustic's everyday goat-skin (*aegis*), people would be apt to speak of any skin-cloak as an *aegis*, regardless of its original species. Thus Athene's snake-skin or owl-skin would equally come to be designated as her *aegis*." The aegis-patterns which he cites and which as breast-plate patterns are historically interesting do not prove his case, without even speaking of the numerous hypothetical assumptions on which this thesis rests.

313 Payne, pp. 80ff.

314 Johansen, p. 157; Plate 41, 5; *Notizie degli Scavi di Antichità*, 1893, p. 470; Payne, figure 23A.

315 *Archäologische Zeitung*, XXXIX, Plate 17, 1; Furtwängler, p. 1716; he also cites (p. 1709) the Hermitage Bronzes, Numbers 342 and 344.

316 Athenagoras, 221Bff., following Alexander of Myndos. The small Asiatic coins from the periods of Valerian I and Gordian III which (in Cilician Laertes and in Seleuceia in Chaldonia) attempted to employ local myths show the Gorgon monster with an aegis-like body and perhaps a bearded, Silenos-like head; cf. Cook, p. 844.

317 On the sharp animal toes belonging to the Gorgon's body it has been remarked that on one Ionian shield which dates no later than 604 B.C. the toes resemble in size the toes of the true wild boar; cf. Wolley, C. L., *Carchemish*, II, London, 1921, Plate 24.

318 The masks of Tiryns seem to represent a transitional being; cf. Karo, G., *Führer durch Tiryns*, Athens, 1934, chapter 17.

319 Cf. the examples in Bieber, M., "Maske," in Pauly-Wissowa, 2113ff. Especially nice is the one opposite the Sileni and the Gorgon, as a shield-image of Achilles and Aias, on the vase of Exekias; cf. Furtwängler-Reichhold, Plate 131.

320 Kerényi, "Man and Mask," pp. 165ff.; *Miti e Misteri*, pp. 453ff.

321 Deubner, p. 233; above, p. 15.

INDEX

1. *Names and surnames, months and festivals*

(Athene, Pallas Athene and Pallas appear on practically every page and thus are not listed here.)

2. *Things, Geography and Topography*